Tales of the
Western Heartland

Other Books By Harry E. Chrisman

Lost Trails of the Cimarron, 1961, 1964, 1975.
The Ladder of Rivers: The Story of I. P. (Print) Olive, 1962, 1965.
Chariot of the Sun, 1964, 1976.
Butcher's History of Custer County, Nebraska (1901). Revised
Edition, 1965, 1976, ed. by Harry E. Chrisman.
When You and I Were Young, Nebraska! (with B. H. Chrisman), 1967,
1976.
The Fighting Railroad Mayor (with Earl Walker), 1968.
Fifty Years on the Owl Hoot Trail: The Story of Jim Herron, First
Sheriff of No Man's Land, 1969, 1975.
Boss Neff in the Texas and Oklahoma Panhandle (1941). Second
edition, 1968, ed. by Harry E. Chrisman.
The 1,001 Most-Asked Questions about the American West, 1982.

Harry E. Chrisman

Tales of the
Western Heartland

*An Anthology of
Cowboy, Scout, Army, Indian, Treasure
and Western True Adventure
Stories*

 Swallow Press/Ohio University Press
Athens Ohio · Chicago · London

A Sage Book of Swallow Press

Library of Congress Cataloging in Publication Data

Chrisman, Harry E.
  Tales of the western heartland.

  Includes bibliographical references.
  1. Frontier and pioneer life—West (U.S.)—Addresses,
essays, lectures.   2. Indians of North America—West
(U.S.)—Wars—Addresses, essays, lectures.   3. Treasure-
trove—West (U.S.)—History—19th century—Addresses,
essays, lectures.   4. West (U.S.)—History—1848–1950—
Addresses, essays, lectures.   I. Title.
F596.C386   1984   978   84-8582
ISBN 0-8040-0857-4
ISBN 0-8040-0858-2 (pbk.)

Design: Cameron Poulter

Cover photo, "The Chrisman Sisters" by Solomon D. Butcher,
1886. (Courtesy Nebraska State Historical Society, the S.D.
Butcher Collection.) *Left to right*: Harriet Susan, "Hattie"
(married Sam Tooley); Elizabeth DeCalmes, "Lizzie" (married Randall Sargent); Lucie "Lutie" (married George Sweeney
and Mr. Miner); Jennie Ruth, "Babe" (spinster, died
in 1974 at age 102).

Contents

Illustrations

Foreword

The Old West receded so quickly before our eyes that the pictures of it and the stories that we wrote about it give only the faintest outline of the events, places and things, and the people who participated in its opening and settlement. Each of us, like the spectators at the scene of an accident, viewed it differently and so reported it. Yet out of the great mass of materials that have been written and painted and drawn to reconstruct for future generations a true picture of the Old West, each reader will select only that part which he regards as pertinent and logical to his own purposes. And perhaps that is best. For no account, however honestly rendered, will ever embrace the magnitude of the story to be told, its splendor and the glory of the simple folk who rode across the western stage at those early periods of American history.

Walt Whitman, one of the greatest to view the scene with his own eyes as he made a trip across the plains in 1878, declined the challenge to "fuse in the alembic of a perfect poem" the true story of the melding of the American West into the national scene. Awed by the vast spaces he viewed, Whitman could only write of the personal exhilaration he felt as he viewed the western grandeur. So it would be impertinent for any writer today to attempt to offer any more than a few brief glimpses of the early West.

In this anthology I have attempted to group a few personalities, some of whom I have known, others I have only written about, who may offer experiences that are new and of interest to readers. Most of the characters are lesser-known figures of western history: trail drivers, settlers, working women and sporting women (both of whom played roles in the western drama), cowboys, feudists, Indian fighters, trailblazers, artists, photographers, inventors, and treasure seekers— all whose lives were most intriguing to me and I hope will be to others. In the variety of their experiences, one gets a small peek into the conflicts and tragedies and the honest good humor that characterized the people of our developing West.

I am indebted to the publishers of *True West, The West, Golden West,* and *Real West* for permission to republish a few of my articles from those publications. My thanks go also to the Denver Posse of The Westerners for permission to extract two articles from their *Brand Books,* 1962 and 1968 issues.

To all who have aided me in the compilation of these stories, my grateful thanks.

HARRY E. CHRISMAN
10245 W. 14th Ave.
Denver, Colorado

Tales of the
Western Heartland

1

The Treasure of the Rifle Pits

The still-undiscovered depot where Gen. Eugene A. Carr buried his treasure during the Indian Winter Campaign of 1868.

He would become a rich man indeed who could find and dig up the treasures buried by the armies of the world in their endless campaigns up and down the lands and across the seas.

Think, for example, of the war supplies abandoned by the Nazis as they fled from Russia, or the war goods Napoleon's army scrapped in the snow that winter of 1812 on its retreat from Moscow. Every GI who served in the last days of the war in the Pacific recalls burying valuable supplies and hardware in the sand or dumping them into the Pacific Ocean. Such treasure is there, buried, sometimes deep, for the army has plenty of manpower to carry rocks and earth and fill up the biggest hole.

One such treasure, and I believe it is still there, though it has eluded me, was buried by the U. S. Army in the winter of 1868–69 during the Winter Campaign against the Plains Indians. This is the treasure of the rifle pits. The location is on Palo Duro Creek, in the extreme northeast corner of Ochiltree County, Texas, and it consists of the materiél of war—rifles, sabers, wagons, hardware, saddles, packsaddles, bridles, and, of course, old glass bottles—buried by the command of Gen. Eugene A. Carr in his underground depot prior to his withdrawal in February and March 1869, and return to Fort Lyon, Colorado Territory, from whence he had come. Two locations are indicated from my research: on Palo Duro Creek, and on Frisco Creek, both in the Oklahoma Panhandle.

I first learned about his episode of history when I was doing re-

2

search on my book *Lost Trails of the Cimarron* in the early 1950s. I had not, at that time, become familiar with Carr's campaign, though of course, like every American, I had heard of Custer's Battle of the Washita since boyhood. Even today many people believe Custer's single engagement and defeat of Black Kettle's camp comprised the whole of that Winter Campaign, and have never known the part General Philip Sheridan, General Sully, General Carr, Colonel Evans, and others played in it.

General Sheridan was at that time in command of the Department of the Missouri and the overall commander of the Winter Campaign. While the campaign itself has little bearing on the treasure of the rifle pits, it was the reason-for-being of the treasure, and is such a little known episode of our western history that it bears retelling.

My informants about the rifle pits were mostly pioneer cowmen of that area, or their sons and daughters who had lived there all their lives and had heard their elders speak of seeing the pits "when on the roundup of '84." These old pioneers had no knowledge of a Winter Campaign being conducted in that region of the Oklahoma Panhandle and north Texas.

One old cowman, speaking of another earlier cowman, said to me, "Oh, he was here when the rifle pits were dug." But though I criss-crossed the country, advertised in the newspapers for information, and had the hand-drawn map provided me by an old friend, I was never able to locate the rifle pits. Even after I had learned that the rifle pits were the abandoned depots of General Carr and Colonel Evans, I was unable to locate them, for the names of streams have been changed since those days when Captain Henry E. Alvord, Tenth Regiment of Cavalry, drew up the detailed map of Carr's campaign.

The inaccuracy of this old army map, together with the lack of time to explore and my move from that region, caused me to abandon my personal search. It had been an enjoyable experience, but I had learned that you needed a truck or four-wheel drive jeep to negotiate those caliche-topped hills and ravines and that you should have a guide along, one who knows his or her way around the wheat and milo fields as well as one who could manage the interminable maze of trails left by the oil and natural gas workers of that area of north Texas and the Oklahoma Panhandle.

To briefly summarize the events of the Winter Campaign it would be well to go back to the Medicine Lodge Treaty of 1867. The failure of that treaty, and the many Indian depredations on the frontier the following spring brought about the War Department's decision to round up the dissidents and put them on reservations or smash them in a winter campaign when the Indians would prefer to sit in the comfort of their lodges along some river. It was a truism that they ranged and raided through the summertime, then holed up along the waters of the Cimarron, Beaver, Canadian, Washita, and Red rivers in the cold weather.

To begin the campaign, Lt. Col. Alfred Sully was ordered to the North Canadian River in September to set up a Camp of Supply, or as they named it, Camp Supply. His forces moved south from Fort Dodge in a twin pincer, designed to clear the Indians from the Crooked Creek area and from the upper waters of the Red Fork of the Arkansas. The following month, Colonel Carpenter scouted the Arkansas River and along the headwaters of the Cimarron and found no large concentrations of Indians in that region. With this good base of supplies prepared at Camp Supply, Bvt. Maj. Gen. (then Colonel) George A. Custer was ordered south in October from Fort Dodge to reconnoiter the Medicine Lodge River area, site of the peace treaty talks the previous year, then to proceed to Camp Supply to rendez-vous with the other forces, including the Nineteenth Kansas Vol. Cavalry.

Meanwhile, at Fort Wallace, Kansas, and at Fort Bascom, in New Mexico, two major groups were being organized and equipped to form the two pincers from the west that would drive all the hostiles to the south and east where Sheridan hoped to meet them with his main force, envelop them, and smash them as a fighting power. This was to happen, it was believed, somewhere on the upper waters of the Washita or Red River. The plan looked good, as all military plans usually do on paper. But one enemy, and the worst one all armies encounter, could not be predicted—the weather.

On a fair day, December 1, 1868, General Carr assembled his command at Fort Lyon, Colorado Territory. This included his Fifth Cavalry Regiment, together with elements of the Tenth Cavalry and service and supply groups, the whole making a force of some 700 men. Three weeks previously Carr had sent Bvt. Brig. Gen. (then Captain) William H. Penrose ahead with troops from the Tenth Cavalry and a mule pack train to march southeast toward the Cimarron on a scout, and from there to the Beaver River, where a junction would be made with Carr's main command when it arrived. This rendezvous was to take place somewhere on the smaller water called San Francisco Creek.

Carr's main force crossed the Purgatoire River, marched south and east slowly as winter weather set in. On the night of 5 December, on Two Butte Creek in a place they named Freeze-out Canyon, a blizzard came down upon them from the north, scattering the horse and cattle herd, tearing down their tents, and completely immobilizing the command. For two days the men were busy digging themselves and their animals out of the snow, reorganizing and trying to find the lost herd of cattle brought along for fresh beef. Only 50 or 60 head of the 150 cattle were ever found. This was a hard blow, for Penrose and his men waiting for Carr were depending on the fresh beef. They had brought only the basic necessities on their mule train. However, the loss of wagon mules in the blizzard and some cavalry horses had also upset Carr's plans, and some of the grain wagons had to be abandoned for lack of animals to pull them.

The weather had dipped to twenty-eight degrees below zero, and both men and animals suffered. Then it moderated, and on the thawing days the wagons moved across the boggy prairie land like cold molasses in January. The wagon teams floundered, and the supply wagons sank hub-deep in the quagmire created on the wet prairie trail by the many heavy wagons and the hooves of the cavalry horses.

The command, so carefully provisioned and equipped, was now short of beef, fodder, and grain for the wagon teams and cavalry horses, and the plains were covered with six to eight inches of snow, making grazing a slow and difficult process for the animals. The general ordered the men put on short rations, for the night at Freeze-out Canyon had taught Carr a valuable lesson which he once later expressed to Frederic Remington, the western artist. Remington had naively inquired of the general what the "unwonted interest in bacon" was all about, for it seemed to be such a continually discussed matter in every Carr command.

5

"The two most important things about a cavalry regiment," Carr told the inquisitive artist, "are the stomachs of the horses and the stomachs of the men that ride them."

Carr's young scout, W. F. Cody, who was to later earn international fame as "Buffalo Bill," was kept riding ahead of the column from ten to twenty miles, looking for Penrose's command, for the snow had obliterated all tracks and only on the high lands where it had blown clear were the scouts able to track well. After making a perilous descent into the Cimarron River valley with the heavy wagons, and crossing the Beaver River, Cody, now riding ahead twenty-five miles, came across three members of the Tenth Cavalry who told him they had become so starved and befuddled that they had started back to Fort Lyon and were now completely lost. Cody and the other scouts backtracked these men and soon made contact with the rest of Penrose's command on San Francisco Creek. They found them in a pitiable state of near starvation, for they had been on quarter rations for more than two weeks. Cody returned to Carr's column and, with Major William H. Brown and two companies of the Fifth Cavalry and their pack mules, returned to relieve the suffering of the Penrose command.

Soon Carr's main column joined Penrose's group along the Beaver River and San Francisco Creek, making a force of approximately 650 men under his command. The hardships that the two units endured had so sapped the strength of both men and animals that General Carr decided to establish a main depot somewhere in the vicinity and proceed on south with the strongest of his remaining forces. It was his plan to establish a junction with Col. Andrew W. Evans, Third Regiment of Cavalry, who was marching east along the Canadian River from Fort Bascom with a command made up of similar elements as his own and with his own provisions and cattle herd.

While Carr sought the junction with Evans in the hope of rebuilding his scanty food stores, Evans, too, had suffered the same attrition from the elements that Carr and his command had undergone. He had lost most of his cattle and was short of fresh meat for his men. His supplies from Fort Union had come late and had been of inferior quality. The 200 Ute and Apache warriors who had started with him and were supposed to augment his command had scattered on the

Cimarron and abandoned the white man's army to its fate, no doubt stealing some of the lost cattle as they departed, since only 62 of Evan's 135 head of beef cattle were ever found.

Colonel Evans continued on down the Canadian River where he established his main supply depot on Monument Creek, a few miles east of the site of Adobe Walls, where the battle between the buffalo hunters and the Indians under Quanah Parker was to be fought six years later.

The Third Cavalry depot was located, as Evans later wrote, "on the 35th Parallel, a little east of its intersection by the 101st Meridian W." This depot was designed to quarter only a few men, including Evans's sick and wounded, but was to hold a good lot of stores. It was dug into the ground and fortified, and revetted with logs and sandbags should an Indian attack occur after Evans's main command, the Third Cavalry, had jumped off on a thirty-day scout to the south where he eventually, on Christmas Day, struck an Indian village and destroyed it. This was the only significant action either he or Carr fought during the entire campaign. Evans took with him about 460 men and more than 500 animals, including cavalry mounts, mule teams, and the remaining cattle. Before leaving he dispatched twenty-two of his supply wagons to Fort Bascom to pick up additional needed supplies.

To the north, on the Beaver River, as the North Canadian is called west of Camp Supply, General Carr dispatched Cody and other scouts to locate a desirable site to establish his own main supply depot. The scouts recommended a place along Duro, or Hackberry Creek (now called Palo Duro Creek), which formed a confluence a few miles north with the Beaver River. The spot is approximately five miles east of the point where the 101st Meridian W. crosses 36 degree 30' of latitude. At that place they found good water, groves of hardwood trees that were useful in the construction of their dugouts and needed for fuel. It was a good winter range, where antelopes were, at least at first, most plentiful for fresh meat, and Cody brought in many for the mess tables.

When Carr had dug in at this depot and fortified it, he then set forth to the south and the Canadian River valley with the hardier elements of his command, leaving behind the sick and lame and weaker members of the command. He expected to form his junction with Colonel Evans and was hopeful that he might borrow rations from the other command. When he reached the Canadian River in December, Carr set up a second depot at a location near the confluence of Mule and Turkey creeks, where they join each other near the Canadian River. Sending scouts both east and west, he soon picked up Colonel Evans's tracks and located the place where Evans had set up his own depot on Monument Creek.

When Cody and his scouts reached the Evans depot there was great rejoicing, for guiding Evans's command, along with several Mexican scouts, was "Wild Bill" Hickok, an old friend of Cody's. At this rendezvous with Evans's scouts, Cody learned that there would soon be a Mexican bull train from the south with a load of beer headed for Evans's depot. The Mexicans had the cold hearts of traders and would offer the beer for sale to the highest bidder, Cody learned. With the instinct of a wolverine on a fresh meat trail, Cody intercepted the train before it reached the Evans command and diverted it northward to the Carr depot (the rifle pits) on the Palo Duro. There, a gigantic Army Beer Bust was held, and those who have never seen or been on one have missed something. It was, Cody wrote years later, "one of the biggest beer jollifications it has been my misfortune to attend."[1] This meeting brought on a general brawl between Cody and his scouts with the Mexican scouts of the Evans and Penrose command who were angry that Carr had made Cody his chief of scouts as a reward for Cody's meritorious services in locating trails, providing food for the command, and giving all the men a general boost in morale during their darkest hours in the cold of that winter. The brawl brought Cody and Hickok on to the Carr carpet, but the general relented, felt the fight was as much the fault of the Mexicans as of the others and let the pair off with a warning.

Carr, after returning to the Palo Duro from his trip to the Canadian, felt the need of information and dispatched five scouts including Wild Bill and Little Geary (Ed Guerrier) to Camp Supply. Other scouts were sent to determine if any Indians remained along the Beaver River, or on Wolf Creek, shown on the old army map as Middle River. The reports were all negative, so it remained for Carr's command to sit and wait, since they were far from the site of the

Indian encampments. And sitting and waiting cost Carr dearly, for although he fulfilled his role in the campaign of holding the western front so the Indians could not escape to the mountains, his entire command was soon threatened with starvation. The winter weather continued, storm followed storm, the snow lay six to eight inches deep over the prairie. Wild game became so scarce that the men were without fresh meat for a week at a time. Forty of Carr's civilian teamsters quit and forfeited their pay. It was now January, and the few supplies that reached him from Fort Lyon were entirely inadequate to his needs.

Luke Cahill, a sergeant with Carr's command who had charge of the headquarters detachment, told of this period of hardship in his story of the Winter Campaign. Carr had by this time been forced to scatter his men up and down the waters of San Francisco Creek and the Palo Duro for the remaining cavalry and wagon animals had eaten out the range near the rifle pits and were required to forage farther and farther away from this main depot. Many of the mules and horses had died from cold and starvation, and the month of February brought only more suffering and greater storms. Wrote Sgt. Luke Cahill later:[2]

> By this time scurvy began to break out among the troops for the lack of vegetables and fresh beef. The doctor said the command was in a fearful condition and that something had to be done and done soon. Gen. Carr and the doctor one evening late called Mr. W. F. Cody and stated the condition the troops were in. The General said, "Mr. Cody, do you think you could get some buffalo meat for the weak and sick men without too much trouble?" Mr. Cody's answer was, "General, that would be a difficult job. Your mules are nearly all in poor condition and the men are little better. Going on but half-rations, six mules could pull but little over the rough prairie, and through the deep snow. The nearest buffalo to this command are at least 75 to 100 miles away, and such an undertaking would take from 12 to 15 days." "But," said Cody, "it could be done with the proper equipment and enough men and mules."

9

The general quickly responded to Cody's statement of his require-ments, and twenty wagons and drivers, a wagon master and twenty infantrymen under the charge of Sergeant Cahill were allotted Cody for the hunt. The detail was provided forage and rations and given the blessing of the general when it set out a few days later for the sheltered areas along the Cimarron and Sharp's Creek, where the best of the winter buffalo range was to be found. Sergeant Cahill wrote later:

> The first day out we could find no water and the mules
> were compelled to lick snow. At the few bare spots on the
> prairie we picked up buffalo chips to make a fire to boil
> our coffee. The snow was frozen so hard we could not
> drive stakes in it to hold our tents up, so we had to spread
> our blankets on the ground and put our tents over them
> so that the wind would not blow the blankets away. We
> had two men on guard, relieving them every two hours.
> Mr. Cody had the same fare that the teamsters and the
> soldiers had, and no complaint had he to make. We
> traveled this way for three days, but on the fourth day,
> about noon, Mr. Cody rode back to the command and at
> the top of his voice shouted, "Boys, we will all have
> buffalo at our banquet tonight! Look yonder, toward the
> northeast."

From a large herd that grazed on the prairie the next day, Cody ran fifty head into the deep snowdrifts in a ravine and there killed all of them. It was a hard and cold job to drag the animals from the drifts with the mule teams, skin and dress them, but the infantrymen under Cahill and the wagon drivers all pitched in and helped. The sergeant wrote: "Cody had the men take out the tongues and brains, saying that the heads were too heavy to haul. We loaded a few wagons and sent the heavy-loaded with his best mules back to the main command with the hope that the supply would relieve the [starving] conditions there, which it did. The men persuaded him to send in the heads also, which he did. They made a fine soup and good eating, and so nothing went to waste, and Cody said that we would now take things easier."

Cody scouted around the following day about twenty miles from the buffalo detail's camp and found another herd of buffalo, and not so much snow. Using two horses, he made a running hunt on this band of buffalo, and shot forty-one head. Exhausted after that day's work, Cody was so used up that he was made to rest. Cahill described the situation: "Cody was very badly jarred from the recoil of the heavy Springfield rifle. His shoulder and breast was a mass of black and blue, so much so it was swollen that he could not put on his coat without help. The buffalo were scattered over twenty miles, and it took us two days to gather them up. All the meat was in fine condition."

Buffalo Bill Cody had killed more than 100 buffalo by this time, according to Cahill, and the meat had saved Carr's command from sickness and starvation. When the buffalo-laden wagons were within four miles of the camps along the streams, General Carr, Captain Penrose, the scouts, including Wild Bill, and most of the officers rode out to meet them. They rode alongside the wagons, shaking every teamster's hand, and when they came to the rear where the weary infantrymen plodded along the snow, they saluted all and shook the hands of most of them, congratulating them on their successful hunt.

That next week was "old home week" in the Carr command, and the general excused every man who had participated in the hunt from pulling night guard for a month. Bill Cody was wined and dined by the officers for the celebrity that he was becoming on the frontier, for he was even at that time exhibiting the characteristics of a great man in the eyes of those who knew him in his best days as an army scout, those men who served alongside him.

From his suite in the Albany Hotel in Denver, 8 March, 1913, in response to a letter from Luke Cahill who later lived at Las Animas, Colorado, Col. W. F. Cody penned the following message to the old army sergeant about the Winter Campaign of 1868–69, still fresh in both men's memories, though the events had occurred 45 years before:

Luke Cahill, sr.,
Las Animas, Colorado

Dear Comrade:

11

Your letter of Feby. 25 was a happy surprise, and your memory perfect. You have mentioned many things in your letter that brought back to me the hardships and privations that we had to pass through in those terrible winters of 1868 and '69. From what I have read of Napoleon's retreat from Moscow in that winter, the expedition of your own was nearly as bad. I remember you very well as a plucky young sergeant of the U.S. Army, butchering the buffalo with your men after I had killed them, and although it was freezing cold to butcher buffalo out in those snowdrifts, not a complaint from you or your men, and if it were not for what we were doing to supply meat for our command, when we were nearly out of rations, there would have been much more suffering among the troops. I wish I could see or get in communication with all the old-timers, especially the scouts and soldiers who actually fought Indians.

Respt. Yours etc., etc.,
W. F. Cody

The worst was over, but there still remained the long march back to Fort Lyon. The great depots were closed and covered over. What materiél could not be carried back (because of the shortage of wagon stock) was left to stir the imaginations of latter-day treasure hunters who seek out the old clevises and wagon bolts and wagon wheels and imperfect, hand-blown whisky bottles and rusty rifles and sabers as energetically as ever did a General Carr or a Colonel Evans search for Indians along those old water courses of the Southwest.

Few of the people who later lived in that area ever heard of Carr's Winter Campaign. The buffalo hunters of the 1870s who came next to that area named the old latrines, dug for sanitary purposes, "rifle pits." And the huge mound that marked the buried depot with its remaining stores completely mystified them. The grass covered all, as it always does, and only the outlines remain to show the agony of Carr's Winter Campaign.

Although the writer has never seen any one of these three depots established by Carr and Evans, one interesting fact about the size of that country was uncovered during my search. One old cowman, Bernard Lemert, who had seen the rifle pits when on the roundup of 1884 said, "It was right down there in Irv Steele's pasture."

After Mr. Lemert's death, I journeyed alone down there one Sunday only to learn that "Irv Steele's pasture" comprised about nineteen sections of prairie land!

On another occasion, an earlier one, I was south of Turpin, Oklahoma, on the south bank of the Beaver River, examining an old formation called "The Spanish Fort." On the west wall of that formation my friend George, who was with me, came across a huge, red sandstone boulder, imbedded in the ground with its face just above the earth surface. On that rock had been carved scores of initials, old cattle brand letters, numerals, and names. The carvings were in such profusion, one atop the other, that they could hardly be separated. Being familiar with the many old brands of the early ranches, I soon traced out Boss Neff's NF, the OX brand of Towers and Gudgell, and others. There were names carved as late as 1945, and there was one dim Spanish engraving with a date that appeared to be 1791.

The rock face so interested us that we returned to the car and got our cameras and a piece of white chalk with which we began tracing out the dimmest of the old lines on the rock face. At this time I had no knowledge of Carr's Winter Campaign, and was searching only for the mysterious rifle pits I had been told about, "where a company of cavalry wintered one time." I had no knowledge that W. F. Cody had ever wintered south of the Union Pacific Railroad in Nebraska, for he was from my home state and that, and his show career, had never placed him in this region as an army scout to my knowledge. So imagine my surprise, delight, and utter disbelief, when chalking out some of the dim lines there appeared the white-chalked signature:

W. F. Cody
USCAYYI

George and I both photographed the signature and discussed the authenticity of it. We were both in agreement that some wag had performed the forgery. We would never know when. In a few more winters it would be completely invisible, like the old signatures and

13

dates are becoming on the inscription cliff at Cold Springs Arroyo, on the Santa Fe Trail, west by north, of this location some 90 to 100 miles.

Yet the feeling persisted that the Cody signature might be authentic for there would be no good reason for anyone to go to the trouble of forging a signature so craftily that it would create an illusion of age by appearing eroded through many years, and especially to do so here, at an isolated spot where scarcely one person in a year or two would ever see it. So perhaps the signature was genuine, not a fraud, since both Cahill's writings and Cody's letter to him authenticate the fact that they were in that section of the country at the time of the buffalo hunt.

So I have had the comforting feeling that despite the fact I never found the rifle pits, never unearthed the treasure from the abandoned war depots of the U. S. Army of 1868, still I did catch a faint whiff of the perfume of the Muse of History as she passed my way at the Spanish Fort on the banks of the Beaver River, that fall afternoon in old No Man's Land.

Notes

1. *The Lives and Legends of Buffalo Bill*, Don Russell, Univ. of Oklahoma Press, Norman, 1960, p. 112 ff.

2. "An Indian Campaign and Buffalo Hunting With Buffalo Bill," Luke Cahill, *Colorado* Magazine, Vol. IV, No 4, August 1927, pp 125–135; ms together with Cody letter to Cahill, March 8, 1913, State Historical Society of Colorado.

2

Loco, the Weed that Almost Won the West

In Spanish the word means "crazy." Its effects on animals bear out the definition.

Ask any old-time rancher in the West if he has *Astragalus mollissimus* on his range and he'll probably look at you through half-closed lids and walk away wondering why you aren't locked up. But mention woolly locoweed to him, and ask about its effect on livestock, and you'll strike up an acquaintance and probably get a dozen firsthand stories about it. For they're one and the same thing, a perennial legume belonging to the pea family.

The effects on saddle horses that became addicted to this weed were fantastic. Early range cowboys—who didn't in most cases own the afflicted animals—found amusement in watching an addicted animal's staggering gait, like a drunken sheepherder heading to the nearest saloon for the final drink.

The ludicrous antics of a locoed horse, leaping five feet into the air to jump clear of its own shadow, brought belly laughs from the cowboys. But a locoed horse falling backward upon an unsuspecting cowboy attempting to mount him for the day's work was funny only for the spectators. And cowboys fought shy of any horse in the remuda that was suspected of being locoed.

My own firsthand encounter with the results of locoweed came when I was a boy in my early teens. We lived at Broken Bow, an old cow town and farming center on the CB & Q railroad in central Nebraska. That summer of 1918 had been a dry one everywhere, but Wyoming was suffering a very severe drought and the cattlemen were shipping out stock cattle to better pasture, after selling down their herds.

My father was a livestock man and he knew of the better pastures in our area, so he helped several of his old friends from Wyoming locate grass there in Custer County, Nebraska. Among these ranchers was A. L. Brock, from Buffalo, Wyoming, who had range on the north fork of Powder River. That summer the Powder was truly a half inch deep, but not nearly a mile wide, as the saying goes. So Mr. Brock shipped several hundred head to our country. I helped father and the men unload them.

The cattle were typical of drought stock: ribs sticking out and their hipbones so high you could hang your hat on them. There were a good many young cows that Brock was saving to build up his future herd. But hungry! My, they were starved, and the hardest kind to drive anywhere, for they ran and picked up anything green and growing alongside the road.

In one of the cars were two saddle horses that Brock had sent along to help move the cattle. One was a bay, the other a small buckskin with a streak down his back.

"Those are good-looking horses," father commented as the two stepped from the car, the buckskin tripping down the cattle chute in the lead, stepping along with the agility of a deer.

"I'll make a present of those horses to any two men you can find who will help move all the cattle I ship in here this summer," Mr. Brock told my father. Dad looked down at me, his eyebrows raised questioningly, and I quickly nodded my head. For though I always had saddle horses available to work with and handle livestock, I had not yet "owned" my own horse.

"My son here rides," father told Mr. Brock. "He can help out."

Brock noticed me for the first time standing there petting the buckskin in my bibbed overalls, red flannel shirt, and worn-out boots.

"He looks like he'll do," the cattleman commented, putting a reassuring hand on my shoulder. For he had no doubt seen, and at some time hired, everything in the way of cowboys there was to be had. So the job was mine!

Mr. Brock told me the buckskin's name was "Spook." I immediately changed it to Buck. But I later learned later why he had been so named.

We moved the first shipment of Brock's cattle to the old Andy Pancake ranch and to Brenizer's ranch, both south of Broken Bow. I then rode Buck for other cattlemen, moving their cattle here and there and earned enough cash to buy a good saddle, for I had always ridden father's and other men's saddles.

On one of these extra cattle drives two other young fellows and I moved 150 head of thin Mexican steers for a butcher, Cornelius Tierney, to pasture east of town. It was nearly twenty miles, a long, hard drive with this thin stock. On the way back our horses were dog-tired and ambled along with their heads nearly dragging on the ground. It was late in the evening, with the sun in our eyes on the western horizon. As we came by the Lon Davis ranch, just outside town, Buck spied a bull in the Davis pasture. Fortunately, I had taken my leg from around the saddlehorn where I had been resting it a few moments before, and it was a good thing. For it was all I could do to stay on Buck with two feet in the stirrups when he cleared by three feet the two strands of barbed wire that fenced the Davis pasture! Then he took off after that bull like a Cheyenne after a buffalo. Though I rode Buck with the usual curbed bit, I might as well have had a scarf tied around his nose, for he was hell-bent and utterly beyond my control.

Any man who has ridden will tell you there is something terrifying about an animal that he trusts going suddenly berserk and running away, the rider being unable to slow down the animal, much less stop it. For there is nothing to do but decide whether you want to sit it out and await the sudden end or to bail out and take your chances on the hard, cactus-covered ground. I elected to ride, but Buck was making such sharp turns and spirals that I was riding with one hand on the horn, the other ahold of the tie straps behind the cantle.

After perhaps two minutes of this nonsense, which seemed more like ten, Buck stopped dead still, spraddle-legged, and just stood there and blowed. I stepped down—quietly—petted Buck and talked to him. But I doubt he heard me for his eyes were wild. I let him stand until he straightened up, and shook himself, then led him back to a gate a few rods back down the fence.

"That damned hoss is locoed," Johnny Siemsen, one of the other boys, said as I rode up alongside of them. I had heard of loco, and we always said of anyone who acted foolish that he was locoed, but this was my first practical experience with the weed. I had learned that a rider has no more control over a locoed horse than he would have mounted on a grizzly bear. When I told father about the incident he warned me against riding Buck so hard.

Buck and I remained pals for two more years. I treated him with greater respect and never rode him hard again. One man who later borrowed Buck and drove several big mules fifteen or twenty miles reported to father, "That Buck is sure a queer actor. Went into a sand blow-out and stood on his head for ten minutes. Couldn't move him."

From what father explained to me about locoweed, and what I later heard and read about it, I learned there was nothing humorous about the weed. For it is a serious threat to livestock.

Locoweed has been found all over the West, from the plains to the mountains. It thrives best in wet years. Locoweed is said to be actually unpalatable to livestock, but once an animal starts eating it he becomes addicted and refuses to eat better forage. The weed is equally poisonous to cattle and to sheep. I have seen cattle, their last year's hair still unshed in late summer, their eyes wild and red-flecked and their bodies thin. These animals had grazed on locoweed over a comparatively long time.

The failure to shed hair, to have extremely long manes and tails, is a certain tip-off to a locoed horse. But by the time they are long-maned and long-tailed their staggering gait and crazy actions are a giveaway, too.

It is only when buying horses in a bunch, buying many head at the same time, that an experienced buyer may be fooled. Yet a horse that is not greatly afflicted can be mistaken for a good animal if running closely in the center of the bunch and not carefully studied by a buyer.

We once bought two carloads of Wyoming and Montana mares and shipped them to Scottsbluff, Nebraska, where father had a large auction sale barn and corrals. We halter-broke those that were un-broken and gentled them for the sales ring. One seven-year-old dappled gray mare was a particularly fine animal. She had been in the middle of the bunch when we looked at them, late one evening, and we had not noticed her other than pausing to observe her fine color and conformation. But when we unloaded them, and father saw the long hair on her belly, he shook his head. The rancher who had sold her had apparently pulled her long mane and tail, but had been unable to curry out the long belly hair that was still unshed.

I took my saddle and laced it on to her. She was perfectly gentle to handle and I mounted her without help. But once aboard she came to life—but only to *back up* against the building that formed one side of the big corral! I dismounted and led her out two or three rods into the corral. This time, when I mounted her, she backed clear across the corral into the fence! I booted her a few times with my spurs until father called to me to stop.

"It's no use," he said quietly, "she's locoed."

We kept her a month or so, but the veterinarian could do nothing to help her, so we had her destroyed. The animals who eat the weed consistently are useless for any sort of work and the debilitating effects of the drug locaine, found in the plant, leave the animal thin and generally with the "blind staggers," as livestock men call it.

At Bridger, Montana, in 1934, we bought several carloads of small, western mares for shipment to Alabama. They were gathered at a ranch south of Bridger and driven to the shipping point at Frannie, Wyoming, about thirty miles distant. The wranglers, all local cowboys, picked mares from the herd to ride, for they were to return on the morning passenger train and there were several mares broken to saddle in the bunch. One young fellow they called Jesse liked a black mare that had what appeared at first glance to be saddle marks on her back where the white hair had grown in over the scar, but which we later learned were old scars from a rodeo surcingle.

When Jesse was finally seated on her, he had a great surprise. The mare, after a strenuous but short struggle trying to throw him, faded like a lily after a funeral and revealed the tell-tale stagger of *locoism*. We turned her out of the stockyard gate, for I didn't want to pay any freight on her kind. She was standing beside the tracks as the freight pulled out, and peering from the window of the caboose I could see a woebegone expression in her eyes as she nickered for the other mares.

But her rodeo days were over, and any other useful work she may have done was forever at an end.

One ruinous effect that locoweed has on an animal is to damage the optic nerve in the eyes. Small objects in the animal's sight then loom up large. A locoed horse will leap over a small mound or clump of grass eight inches high and clear it by several feet.

Al Olive of Dodge City once told me of an experience his father, the famous Print Olive, had with a locoed horse. Al was nine or ten when this happened, but he still chuckled about it when he related his father's experience of seventy-five years before.

"Father traded for this colt up on the Walnut, north of Dodge," Al recalled. "Got him from Mudge, who had range up there. He saddled the colt one morning for a trip to Ravenna. The old Texas cow trail passes near there, and when father came to cross those ruts, about sixty feet of them in width, damned if that colt didn't try to jump all of them at the same time. Father told us later that when the colt jumped the first six ruts he was four feet high; on the second set he was eight feet in the air. On the last ruts Father said the hoss must have been twelve feet high, though he didn't stop to measure. He always said that little roan gelding put up a better show crossing the Texas trail sidewise then he ever had seen one do riding it lengthwise! Yes, there was lots of locoweed there in '85, and that colt was full of it."

This woolly locoweed that causes such disturbances grows from eight to eighteen inches in height. It has large, tough, alfalfalike roots that it sinks deep into the earth, so it is no easy task to rid a range of it. The new poisons kill it, but it is a persistent seeder and sometimes comes right up again from the roots, even after a grass fire. It grows in stout clumps that are frequently two feet in diameter, and I have seen it grow in profusion along dry creek banks and in arroyos and ravines where it seemed to be well-protected. But it also thrives on the flat plains.

The individual plant has about a dozen stems from each of which sprout leaves, in pairs, on each side of its woolly stalk. The stem appears to be coated with small, white hairs, hence the name "woolly." When the plant blooms, it casts forth many bluish lavender-colored blossoms quite in contrast to its green leaves. Woolly

Locoweed is not dissimilar to the sweet-smelling lupine that flowers around the lagoons and low areas in the central Nebraska hill country and elsewhere.

Actually, locoweed is best fought by persistently grubbing out the plant, eight or ten inches in depth and burning the stalks to kill all root and seed. On small areas this is possible, and I have helped rid a ranch yard of it in this manner. But where range land several square miles in extent must be treated, a solution of commercial poison, about one and a half pounds per acre, is recommended. Some ranchers have sprayed their land from airplanes. Others treat the weed from the ground, which is probably the surest method, for individual attention can be given the badly infested and hidden areas in ravines and canyons that may be acting as a seedbed for its spread.

Not much appears to have been written abut locoweed during the Texas trail-driving days, yet cattle and horses undoubtedly did come across infested areas while moving northward on the Chisholm Trail and the Western Cattle Trail. Probably not too much was then known of its effects on livestock, for there were the more obvious outbreaks of screwworm, tick fever, and other diseases and pests like heel flies to worry and concern drovers and their cowboys. The daily movement of the trail herds would also take them away from locoweed-infested areas, so the animals probably failed to contract the addiction as they would if grazing permanently on an infested range.

"Old John" Kirkpatrick, of Cody, Woming, who came up the Western Trail as a boy of sixteen years once told the writer of finding locoweed addiction beginning in a bunch of young geldings he had bought and was training for roping and cutting horses. He soon traced the weed to a small spring in some nearby hills. He grubbed out the bushes with a shovel. Only one horse was permanently affected, and he had no more trouble with the weed. Old John thought that the seed had been windborne into the country for there had been no addiction among livestock in that area of northwest Wyoming at the time.

Among cattle, locoweed addiction is less noticeable than among saddle horses, for little more is expected of cattle than that they graze, get fat, and be shipped to market. Many cattle on the far northern ranges carry long, shaggy hair even in late spring and early summer, so this telltale sign found among the horses is less meaningful in beef herds.

It is also true that men working cattle are not with them so constantly as they are with their riding horses, sometimes seeing the cattle only a few times each year, and then from a distance. One old cowman told me, "I never look for the signs of addiction in my cattle; just watch for the weed on the range and keep the cattle away from it."

Among the saddlestock, the animals must have a high degree of intelligence and are expected to be fleet of foot and agile in their work at roping or cutting in the corral. Therefore, the slightest effect from browsing on locoweed is easily detected. An animal that does not respond quickly to the touch of the reins, knees, or spurs, and fails to keep its attention on the work at hand is instantly suspect. By the time the hair is shaggy or the gait staggering it is already too late to save the horse.

After only a few weeks munching on the weed, a young horse will already suffer some optical illusions that can be detected. A season or two on the weed, and its nervous system and brain are damaged. Sometimes, as in the case of my little saddle horse, Buck, the animal is rescued before it is entirely too late and can be useful if not used too hard. No doubt Buck had been valued and appreciated by Mr. Brock and his men or he would never have been saved by them.

A whole passel of deadly poisonous or slightly toxic plants, legumes, and grasses have been identified all over the West. There are ergot, arrowgrass, woody aster, brome snakeweed, common horsetail, Texas croton, hemp dogbane, poison hemlock, Texas buckeye and others. Some have brought serious loss to livestock. Others are less toxic and have little effect on stock. Each appears to have its dangerous season, but livestock browing on better, tastier forage seem to browse right over it. Some of these plants are best suited for the southern climate, some for the northern.

The wonderful, but common, chokecherry bush, which provided pioneers with its sweet, red fruit from which no better jam can be made, also manufactures in its leaves the poisonous hydrocyanic acid, deadly to livestock.

Although I spent my boyhood years on a range in the hill country that was infested with chokecherry bushes, I never heard of an animal of any kind getting sick from eating chokecherry leaves, much less dying from it. Though a cousin from Missouri once described a chokecherry as "a seed with skin stretched over it," no one in our country would have said a word against the chokecherry bush, any more than we would have defamed the gooseberry bush from which came our delicious gooseberry pies! The cattle just didn't browse the chokecherry leaf, it appears, probably because of the succulent buffalo and bluestem grasses which grew in such abundance.

Cases of cattle poisoning have been reported over the Great Plains country from eating the gambel oak, called scrub oak, which thrives over the West. The period of danger appears to be spring, especially when late frost has nipped the buds and leaves, turning them black. Normally, scrub oak is considered good livestock browse. The poison, in its case, is reported to be tannic acid.

The Department of Agriculture lists seven types of locoweed known to produce the symptoms heretofore described and termed *locoism*. But this one species, woolly locoweed, is representative of the rest for our purposes. The woolly locoweed that most livestock men can recognize on sight always seems to be the most talked-about and unpopular weed on the western range. For many a fine saddle horse, the pride of a rancher and turned out to pasture for a few weeks in the off-seasons, has returned to the corral listless, sometimes tumbling, a victim to the poison charm. It is a sad and pitiful sight to see a fine animal ruined by the noxious weed.

Of all poisonous vegetation, no other has caught the popular fancy or has been dealt with more thoroughly in western literature than woolly locoweed. Fortunately, locoweed is coming under the control of ranchers, and this toxic plant "that almost won the West" may soon be browse for only the dodo bird. And it will not be greatly missed.

3

The Hired Girl of the Great Plains

She introduced German *strudl*, Russian *kulitch* and Bohemian *kolachy* to American diets.

As the tide of immigration flowed from the wooded areas of the Mississippi Valley westward on to the Great Plains, men's and women's duties began to change to match the needs of the new economy being brought about by Plains farming. With few heavily wooded areas now to clear before plowing and planting, the man's work became somewhat easier. Once he had plowed the buffalo sod and planted his crop, his work became lighter.

After his sod house had been laid up, the well dug, and sheds and corrals erected, the man of the family actually found himself with a little leisure time. His animals helped him greatly, and the incipient farm machinery revolution played an important part in lifting that burden of ages—heavy farm labor—from his sweating back. Furthermore, he usually had the help of a hired man or neighbor to lighten the load when the work was too great.

Within the home, however, the old-fashioned wood and coal range, the kerosene lamp, the churn, and the washboard were still queen for their day. Dishes were still washed and dried by hand. The chickens were watered and fed by hand. Milk was skimmed for its cream, then placed in crocks and jars for future use and disposal. All these tasks, and many more, meant that a great burden of farm work fell on the tired shoulders of the farm wife and mother. With all these duties, she was usually still enlarging her family at the rate of a new baby every twelve to eighteen months. Small wonder that her life expectancy was short.

On nearby farms—but sometimes quite distant in the early days—lived other families, frequently with several older or half-grown girls. Occasionally a family would have four or five girls, with one of the older ones wanting to get away from her own home to meet other people, and perhaps to find a suitable hired man who would make her a good husband. And so the social and economic needs of the exhausted farm wife found its answer in this older neighbor girl who wanted work "away from home," and the farm wife took into her employ a "hired girl."

Once employed, the hired girl's work pattern became not too different from that of her employer. There were few Ladies on the western frontier in the eighties and nineties, especially on the farms and ranches. The stock that had emigrated westward was seeking land, not social activities. These middle- and lower-class immigrant women, although not society folk, were from a polite society of their own classes. So at first they handled the cowchips for the fires with gloved hands. Later, without donning gloves, they faced up to handling the chips with bare hands, afterward carefully washing the fingers. But water was scarce, and after a year or two of living in a Plains home, they found themselves stuffing chips into the firebox with one hand while they pulled the soda biscuits from the oven with the other, quite unconscious of their new attitude.

They had become Westerners. And their sons, eating at the "second table" were learning how to conserve water for dishwashing by "just eating off of pa's plate."

When the railroads crept west and changed "holding down a claim" into farming for a profit, the era of the hired girl bloomed. "Working out," as it was termed, enjoyed little popularity in homestead days when there was no money reward and the hired girl labored for "board and keep." But when an assured money income became possible for the farmer and his wife, they were happy to share a small portion of it with a hired girl to help lift the burden from the mother's back.

Usually, the presence of a hired girl in the home gave the farm family the needed time to add those little extras that made the home and its surroundings brighter and cheerier. A little flower garden soon appeared. New rugs for the floors were woven. Patchwork quilts for the beds were pieced and handwoven coverlets created. More clothes for the children could be made, and the home became pleasant for all members. Many of these old handicrafted items that were a part of the luxuries a hired girl's presence in the home helped to make possible are so valued today that antiquarians search eagerly in the shops of the nation for them.

The social position achieved by the hired girl in her time was both unique and envied. She was regarded more as a dependable older daughter or maiden aunt than as a servant. She ate at the first table in many homes; she slept in one of the family beds—often with one of the smaller children. She remained in the parlor with the family when visitors came. She was respected by all family members, and she often rewarded her co-worker and closest companion, the farm mother, with her undying love and devotion.

In the writer's own family, Mandy Coffman was a beloved name, a Nebraska hired girl who helped our mother through many difficult times.

Another former Nebraska resident, the late Russ Langford, of Lookout Mountain, Colorado, related to the writer how, when he stood at the graveside of his own mother during the funeral services, a former hired girl of their family stepped over to his side, pressed his hand in hers and spoke quietly to him.

"Your mother was my mother, too, Russ," she told him. "No kinder or more blessed woman ever lived."

Sometimes the hired girl did actually become, through marriage, a member of the family. In the beautifully told story of her family's life on an Oklahoma homestead, Catherine Ward Allen, Pond Creek, Oklahoma, related in her book, *Chariot of the Sun*, how her mother's loyal helper and good friend, a hired girl named RuAmy Jane Hart, became her beloved stepmother following her mother's death. This stepmother raised Franklin Ward's children, two girls and a boy, aged two, five, and eight, respectively. She added to this nucleus of a family four more stalwart sons. To all of these children the young woman who had been "hired girl" soon became "Mother RuAmy."

Another grand lady from Liberal, Kansas, that the writer knew in her late eighties was called, by neighbors and friends alike, "Aunt Betty." She had worked as a hired girl for many neighbors and had served their families so well that the youngsters in most of the families called her "Aunt Betty," never realizing that she was entirely unrelated to them! Aunt Betty Lemert's memory is cherished by all the people of her community today.

And so it went, and as many nationalities from abroad fell into the American melting pot in the Midwest and West, their young women "worked out" as hired girls, bringing their languages and Old World customs as an added cultural facet to the plains youth in whatever geographical area they settled. The Irish, the Germans, the Dutch, the Scandinavians, the Bohemians, and others were soon integrated as Americans. In that process of assimilation, they contributed many beneficial native customs, transplanted an ocean away from their native land.

The strange new names—Annie O'Flannagan, Mary Sogol, Rosie Olsen, Ruby Ingstrom, and Katrinka van Volkenstein—brought amusement to the children. But they soon loved these young women of foreign extraction as members of their own families.

Sometimes the hired girl spoke a very broken English, and this brought snickers from the children. But never did the mother or the grandmother in the home permit the children to laugh rudely in the hired girl's face or make fun of her. For this was a process in which strange languages and stranger customs were being assimilated by both sides. The so-funny expressions soon became a part of our families' language, "Americanized," and the contributions to the American idiom brought over by the immigrants from foreign shores are now recognized by all lexicographers.

In the writer's own family, "Kommen sie an" and "Sitzen sie down" are familiar meal-time announcements, as well known to us as "Come and get it" was to our fathers and mothers. They are the contribution of a pretty German girl, Rachael Preszler, Jamestown, North Dakota, a *sis madchen* who came to the United States in 1879.

Contributions to western cooking made by the hired girl are so many they will never be fully appraised. Her work in the frontier kitchens brought many recipes from foreign shores into intimate relationship with the hungry stomachs of plains dwellers. Old world cuisine—Russian *kulitch*, German *strudl*, Bohemian *kolachy* and the delicious Scotch scones—has long been known for its appeal to jaded appetites. Here, on the fading frontier, with its bread-bacon-beef-coffee diet, the new recipes from the Old World, such as Irish stew, Scandinavian *lefsa*, Polish sausages, French pastries, and Italian spaghetti, found great appeal. Today, all these foods and scores of others have earned a respected place in our kitchens, making the American diet probably the most sophisticated, and certainly the most cosmopolitan, in the world.

Along with these succulent dishes the hired girl also learned to prepare the foods native to the land. Fried jackrabbit, antelope loins, roast beef and roast prairie dog, lambsquarter greens picked fresh in late spring, and buttered hominy were all prepared by her hands.

She also soon developed a taste for those strange farm and ranch dishes such as headcheese from the hog, scrambled calves' brains, tripe and cottage cheese. In season she picked and dressed—and oftimes shot—prairie chicken and quail, and such migratory wild fowl as Canadian geese and the mallard ducks, as they came down from Canada to their winter homes each fall.

In the spring and summer the hired girl also labored in the vege-table garden, and in the fall she helped to can the produce she had grown for the family. One young Dutch girl who could hardly make herself understood in English taught a farm family a word they long remembered—*sauerkraut*. She put down a ten-gallon crock of the chopped cabbage, and taught the family how to combine wieners with it to make a delectable dinner dish.

The experiences of the hired girl were sometimes unique and humorous. Many such incidents have been repeated down through the years by family members who treasure the little stories. Mrs. Opal Harber, formerly of the Denver Western Library staff, tells of a family who entertained a large group of young people at their farm home one night.

The hired girl, though welcomed, begged off and retired early, since she had put in a long, hard day at work.

During the course of the night a terrible rain and electrical storm came up, forcing the guests to remain at the farm home for the night, since there was a swollen river to ford. About two o'clock in the morning when the party spirit was wearing thin and the light refresh-ment had given out, the group was hungry enough to want a meal. They decided to play a trick on the hired girl, whom all knew well.

Two of the girls were sent to awaken her. They told her it was six o'clock, and time to prepare breakfast, since the farm wife was indisposed that morning. The hired girl quickly arose and dressed in the dark as was her habit. She went to the kitchen and prepared an enormous breakfast of cereal with thick cream, hot biscuits, ham and bacon, pancakes, fried eggs, potatoes, and a gallon or two of coffee.

The guests assembled at the kitchen table and enjoyed a hearty breakfast before revealing to the hired girl that it was then only three o'clock! Everyone enjoyed the joke, including the hired girl, who, refreshed by her night's sleep, stayed up and with her guitar became the new life of the party!

All hired girls were not by any means patterns of perfection. One farm wife related how a fraulein of their time, fresh from the old country, came into the parlor one day while she was entertaining members of her Literary Club, among whom were two very cultured ladies who had recently come from the East. The hired girl swept into the parlor without invitation, her face flushed and streaked with perspiration, a dishpan filled with the remains of a chicken clutched in her hands.

"Mrs. Hazelton," she inquired, without a second glance at the visitors, "vot shell I do mit dese checken guts?"

But the hired girl's duties were not all concerned with just cooking and housekeeping. She worked some outdoors, she trimmed the Christmas tree, she helped tie the quilts, and made the children's valentines.

Because she labored so closely with the mother and daughters of the household, she learned the American manners and social graces. The farm wife helped her, and she improved her mind by reading the ladies' magazines, books, and newspapers that found their way into the household. The personal services the hired girl rendered to the family brought important advantages to her that did not always accrue to her counterpart who worked in the city at similar tasks, such as waiting tables in restaurants and cooking and housekeeping.

The wages paid her, though relatively little in cash, were not all that was exchanged for her labor. She received board and room, light, fuel and laundry, all of which workers in trade had to purchase. Her work required no capital investment, no typewriter or sewing machine. She was not required to have any particular educational achievements, and she spent nothing for transportation to and from her work.

Professor Lucy Salmon of Vassar College once reported that a wage of $3.25 per week made it possible for a hired girl to save up to $150 annually. This, of course, is drawing the noose too tight and shows a poor understanding of the hired girl's needs. But there *was* an opportunity to accumulate a nest egg that young women working in the cities did not always have. And we all know young women today drawing salaries up to $200 and more per week who save nothing from a year's work!

One hired girl, Rosie Olsen, well known to the writer's family and whom we all loved and respected, came from a small farm in a central Nebraska county. When she married she and her husband moved to the Sandhills country where they took out a homestead. After a few years of hard labor and little progress, the husband quit and left for another community, leaving the wife and their small children on the claim. The ex-hired girl hung on as long as she could, but when the children became hungry she left the claim and moved to the nearest small town on the railroad. But she kept title to the claim. In town she obtained a job washing dishes in a small restaurant. Being a good cook, and a most willing worker, she had soon established herself as the head cook. A few more years and she bought the restaurant! Then she added a dance hall for the young people of the area.

With the help of a sympathetic banker in another town, she bought a hotel in her town and put in a dining room. Soon her places were the major attraction for the ranch families and cowboys for a hundred miles around. She prospered, made a good home for her children and educated them. Today her name is esteemed throughout the Sandhill area of Nebraska.

Those of us who knew her when we were children, who were cared for by "Rosie," loved and adored her and will never forget her sweet disposition, her rugged Swedish strength of character, and her iron will and determination to always do what was right.

A few thoughtless mothers and householders may have treated their hired girls shabbily, but those mothers and farm wives who came from better families and brought more cultivated manners to the grasslands of the West generally treated the hired girl with all the civility and respect shown the other members of their families.

News of bad treatment of a hired girl traveled fast, and a farm woman who used her hired girl badly or overworked her was forced to pay a much higher wage, and usually got the type of help she deserved.

The hired girl of the West never knew what it was to stand and wait, as her eastern counterpart did, for a "gentleman" to take off his hat and coat and hand them to her to put away. For all ranchers and farmers, unless ill or crippled, were able and willing to remove and hang up their own clothing. And the hired girl had more important things to do than keep her employer's clothes free of dust and lint!

Although the girls had no labor standards, they toiled and ate alongside the family members, doing what had to be done. If the family was a large one, there was much cooking, washing, and bed-making. In most western homes the children were taught self-reliance and were able to help with those tasks. Only the babies demanded, and received, full attention.

The hired girl had more than enough to keep her occupied. She cranked both the ice cream freezer and the cream separator. She either rubbed the clothes on the washboard or pushed the handle of the primitive wooden tub washing machines of that day. She turned the wringer handle to help dry the clothes, and she pinned the clothes on the outside lines both winter and summer.

Many a hired girl heard the friendly warning made by the housewife, "Be careful, Carrie, and don't crack the frozen clothes when you take them from the line!"

Water was carried long distances from the windmill to fill the reservoir at the end of the Majestic range so the family could have fresh water daily for cooking, for bathing, and for dishwater.

Most of these young women who worked out were from poor families. At first, many worked out for board and room, for their families were too poor to feed them. Others left home because of family misunderstandings and difficulties. One such young girl, Harriet Emmaline Upjohn, at seventeen left her farm home in Kansas because her stepfather insisted that she herd cattle afoot. Emmaline was a proud and sensitive child, very pretty, and at the time keeping company with the son of a rich cattleman who ranched nearby. When she made her decision to leave home, she told no one about it; she just went to a nearby farm and started to work in the kitchen.

Emmaline worked on cattle and sheep ranches, then found herself employed as a waitress in a hotel at WaKeeney, Kansas. She met another young man whom she loved, and they married and raised a family in California.

The work habits of the hired girl of that day produced the climate for good health and regularity of habits. The work introduced into her life during her employment was such that it trained her completely for motherhood and the responsibilities of bringing up her family in a well-ordered home.

The hired girl of yesterday became the grandmother of today. She faithfully performed her duties to her employer, her country, and her God. From a lonely existence working in other women's homes, helping to feed and clothe their children, she built her own sympathetic and understanding character. When she married, she helped to make a better world for her husband and their children. She gave an honored name to a humble profession, and she is still revered in the West, by all who knew her and shared her life.

Other young women on the frontier—the dance hall girl, the Harvey girl, the cowgirl and the school ma'am—have heard their praises in song and story and on film. But not this young woman who was called simply, *the hired girl.*

So it is fitting and proper that she should be recognized for this part she played in the winning of the West, and for the many womanly attributes she possessed and passed on to the younger generation.

As Walt Whitman might have expressed it, "Let us sing the belated praise of America's Hired Girl—the Unsung Heroine of the West!"

4

The Sierra Madre Treasure

Old Sebastian made a million . . . and then he lost his luck.

Frequently a writer follows a trail to an end but discovers material not pertinent to his research. That happened to me while researching the life story of an old Arizona cowman who brought cattle out of Mexico during the revolution. At Yecero, Sonora, Mexico, I learned of an old-timer who had known my man. (He asked me to withhold his name, so I will just call him Old Sebastian.) I sought him out and was disappointed to find he could provide little information about the cowman, or his activities in Mexico. But the old-timer's mind was filled with lore of placers, stopes, gold, quicksilver, and manganese. Here is the story he told me.

Down in Sinaloa, the Sierra Madre is high, and tough to climb, for the trails run along the cliffs at dizzy heights. Even with the mule packs it is difficult to reach the top. But on one high divide there was a placer that gave up gold in fine grains like that of wheat, and even of corn grain size.

When we went up there, after the turn of the century and when the revolution was just beginning, we took along two dry washers. They blow away the dirt and leave the gold dust and iron-coarse gold, which we gathered in a pan with quicksilver. The Tarahumara Indians helped screen the gravel and turned cranks on the washers.

33

We were fortunate. In three months we had caught on the screens five kilos of placer gold.

But this was expected. What I want to tell you about is the treasure we never expected to find when we went up there. There were three of us, besides the Indians who helped. I was the only Anglo, for the other two of my party were Mexicans.

While we worked, those Indians told us of three other men who had worked this rich placer long before us. They were there for nearly two years, one older Indian told us, and they had taken much gold from the placer—that was well known to the Indians who helped them. These men had also worked a good placer high up on the mountain on a very difficult trail, alongside a swift mountain stream. They lived in a large cave, near the upper placer, one old Indian said. Later, after them, there were earth tremors that created landslides on the trail. After that, few men tried to ascend there.

When I questioned the Indians about the cave, they did not want to talk. When I asked for guides to take me up there they would not go. One younger Indian, Chessee, the son of the old Indian who seemed to know the most about it, and who had worked there, had been to the upper placer just the year before. We asked Chessee and his father to guide us, but the old man was fearful and would not go.

He said that the three miners who had worked the upper placer had taken their gold, all of it, into the cave and hidden it. They had built a heavy wooden door at the entrance, so it could be locked up. The cave was ventilated and they could have a fire in cold weather. One day a bandit, Bates Belanco, and three other armed men came up the trail with good horses and pack mules. They had heard of the gold through some of the Indians at the foot of the mountain.

The bandits caught the miners eating in the cave and killed them, leaving the bodies where they fell. They scared all the Indians away. Then they searched for the gold. Though they stayed three days, they never found the hiding place of the *grande cache*. The Indians knew they were there, and avoided the bandits, for they knew Belanco and his thieves would torture them to death trying to learn where the gold was hidden, even though the Indians did not know.

When the bandits finally left, the Indians waited several days, then crept back up the trail to the cave. They saw the bodies of the three dead miners in the cave entrance. But their chief told them they would also fall dead if they entered the cave. So they closed the door and left. Chessee's father said that now only the ghosts of the dead lived there, and these ghosts would permit no man to live who entered the cave!

Though we asked him again, Chessee's father would not guide us to the cave. But Chessee agreed to take us, if he was not made to enter the cave. To this we agreed.

That following week, we left off our work at the lower placer and the three of us, accompanied by Chessee, started up the trail. We carried provisions for a week's stay, but took no pack animals, for the trail was too steep and the footing too poor for the animals. It was a long, hard climb, and we used ropes in two places to ascend precipices where the trail was gone and the cliffs were most difficult to climb, but we reached the cave on the second day.

The next morning we stood before the heavy wooden door which was still in good condition and held together with iron straps. The door was not locked, and opened easily. As we peered into the dimness ahead, we could see that the interior was exactly as Chessee's father had described it. And there at the entrance were the remains of the three miners, the bones still carrying the dried skin around them. Small rodents had chewed and stolen most of the clothing on the bodies. We piled stones over the miners' bodies and left them where we found them after erecting a wooden cross over the remains. Then we started searching for the gold the miners were said to have hidden.

Within two hours I came on to a four-inch iron pipe, buried in the ground within the cave, off to one side, where a small niche in the wall had been made for a bed. With pickax and shovels we began digging for the pipe was in a vertical position. For a while all we could unearth was the rounded sides of the pipe, but at a depth of six inches we could see where another part had been joined, and on the cap of this part was a slot in the cap, which was screwed onto the threads of the main pipe. I could see in an instant that this concealed part was, or had been, used to fill the pipe that was still below the surface. Digging on down two feet below the floor level, we came to a place where the pipe had been joined to a washtub, with an iron cover, below. From the remains of that rusty washtub, we took ninety thousand dollars in placer gold, much like what we had been mining at our lower placer, but with many larger grains, and a few nuggets of pea size!

We had agreed on an even division of all gold we took from the Sierra Madre, although it was my money that had financed the expedition and my two companions' knowledge of the country that led us to the lower placer. I paid both Chessee and his father well for their guidance and information, and gave them a portion to help guide us off the mountains and to the railroad. I cautioned them to keep quiet, even to their people, the Tarahumaras, with whom they would eventually divide their shares, until we were clear of the country.

When we three arrived at Culiacan, I had a portion of the gold assayed and sold some of my share to the Banco Nationale of Mexico. Then I took a train to the United States.

At San Francisco I transported the remaining gold dust to the Reduction Works across the bay and had it melted and converted into bars of five pounds each, troy weight. There were ten of these bars made.

That fall I embarked for Calcutta, India, where I had friends who were in the gold-buying business, and I sold the bars at a premium price, taking pound notes on the Bank of England in return. In London I exchanged the notes for U.S. currency and came to New York, where I spent several weeks, after having traveled completely around the world.

I could go on and on and relate how, from this ninety thousand dollars we originally found in the gold cache, and from our own placer work, my share eventually made me worth more than one million dollars by 1937. But this would only cause me to relate the painful facts of how I lost all this money within a few years on speculations, and by family betrayals, a subject too painful to me to discuss.

I can say that today I am past eighty years of age, and I hope to make another fortune, before I "cash in my chips," by searching for El Dorado. I have lived in Mexico now for many years. I like the people here, and I am of a firm faith in the great future of this country, especially in the development and discovery of its enormous mineral reserves. Gold, silver, lead, copper, quicksilver—all these metals and others will be prized more and more as time passes. So I bid all prospectors and treasure seekers to take heart, and keep looking.

Good luck to you all!

5

I. P. (Print) Olive, Texas Cowman

A new light upon a controversial western character who was neither all good nor all bad.

Most Westerners know something of the life of I. P. (Print) Olive, who was killed at Trail City, Colorado, on Monday, 16 August, 1886.[1] It has been impossible to alter the date although many writers have otherwise changed the details of his murder, and not a few have taken the liberty to completely falsify the events leading up to and surrounding Olive's death. As a result of such work in the literary field, millions of copies of national and regional magazines, newspaper articles, books, and papers that deal with this Texas cattleman's murder have achieved an unbelievably low score for accurate reporting of the matter.[2]

What is most surprising about these tales is that the facts have always been readily available should anyone have cared to inquire into the event. Yet few writers have cared to delve into the primary research materials for the truth about Olive's death—or his life, for that matter. So the early *misinformation* that was published about Olive and his affairs has been enlarged upon until an ordinary tough, courageous, independent, old Texas cowman has become the whipping boy for many western writers searching for a villain to give color, if not credence, to their stories.[3]

In a sense, these writers may be excused. We western writers are pretty much alike, and our problems quite similar. We have jobs to hold down; our research work is usually carried out whenever and wherever we can spare an hour or so for it. If we uncover an old chip of information, especially one published contemporaneously with the event we are studying, we grab for it. Oftimes we accept it as gospel truth without applying elemental reason to studying its facts. It helps us temporarily. But it frequently does great damage to others—sometimes to the family of the subject studied. For error, however early it may have been published, is still error. Actually many photos, news items, court records, and manuscripts have been so tampered with and altered in the years since the old events occurred that all should be suspect to the alert researcher.[4] For even then, error finds many ways of creeping into our work.

There are, of course, some writers who twist and bend every fact within their reach to make everything conform to their prejudgment of the historical event. But we need not be concerned with them at this time, for "by their works you shall know them."

My point is that had the past research of the life of I. P. Olive and his family been conducted with the honesty and historical perspicacity with which most historical research has been carried on, then he would have emerged as a far different character than this, and I quote, "Tyrant of the Plains," or "Manburner," or "One Man Mafia of the Plains." For just elemental honesty and a frank look at the trial records of his murderer would have prevented anyone with a claim of any sort as a "historian" from telling that wild and crooked yarn about an upright and honest young cowboy "outdrawing" Olive in true TV and motion picture style while the elderly gunman fell on his own weapon! But so much for the lies or honest mistakes—if such they were—of the past. Let us hope that even in this brief paper we have apprehended some of them.

What is less known about Mr. Olive's career in Colorado is that a decade before his death at Trail City he was numbered among the earliest cowmen in northeastern Colorado. The Olive brothers, of which Print Olive was the ramrod, were sharing range on the North Fork of the Republican with other cowmen in 1876. His neighbors were J. W. Bowles; the 21 Outfit, a Texas group; Thomas Ashton; the Reeck Brothers, Charles and Frank; the Bar T Ranch, and several others.[5] It was a crowded range in a drought year on that stream, and the Olive brothers had only the one, 3,000-cow herd wedged in between other cattle outfits along the creek. Even with the cattle

39

grazing back ten miles from water, south of the river, it was poor range.

But who were the Olives? Why were they here on the Republican Fork, so far from their native range?

The Olive brothers were sons of a pioneer Texas cowman, James Olive, who registered his brand in Williamson County as early as 1850. Print or Prentice, the oldest boy, began work on the "cow hunts" at the tender age of eight years, riding the bell mare. Soon he was doing a man's work in the saddle, roping the *cimarrones* in the brushy thickets and burning into their hides his father's old "pound" brand, (LB) as it was called. At age twenty-one, in 1862, Print entered the Confederate service. He stayed through the war with his unit until the final surrender, having served in Texas, Louisiana, Mississippi, and Tennessee, with honor.

Back home, in 1866, a hardened veteran, he again took up the cow work with his brothers, Jay, Ira, Bob, and Marion. All held registered brands in the county. Soon they realized that only by savage warfare against the scores of rustlers that infested the region could they hold their herds, gather more cattle, and turn them up the cattle trails to market. By 1876, Print had been critically wounded twice by the region's rustlers.

"There have been more men killed in Williamson County this year than were killed in the war," wrote the editor of the *Austin Statesman* in 1876. In August of that year a band of twenty or thirty rustlers raided the Olive Pens, killing Print's brother, Jay, and wounding Print and other Olive cowboys. Print had just been called back from the Colorado drive in time to witness this battle and engage in it. He was now convinced that they must leave Texas for good. But before leaving he and Bob performed a task they had each sworn to do: they killed the chief of the rustling gang and his lieutenant.[6]

Meanwhile, in the north, Ira Olive wintered the cow herd at Corral Canyon, an eroded area on a dry streambed where floodwaters flow down from the hills to the south into the Republican Fork, near Haigler, Nebraska.[7] This location was where Ira Olive killed the Mexican *vaquero*, Leon, who had pulled a knife on him. Leon's body was buried near the Olive Pens; later it was taken up and moved to their new ranch headquarters location upstream near Wray, Colorado.

When the writer visited this latter location, in 1958, Mr. Fred Count, the owner of the land, told how the folklore mentioned "one of the Olive's" being killed and buried there, beneath the giant cottonwood trees that now grace the area. It is possible that these huge trees were planted by the Olives, but there was hardly a tree along the river in 1876. Prior to visiting Wray, Colorado, the writer had no knowledge that the Olive Brothers had ranged cattle in this area. In my files was a letter from Mr. Diss, president of the National Bank of Wray telling me, in answer to a request, that there was a place called Olive Lake near the town of Wray. The lake, I found, had been created about 1898. The dam had washed out about 1925 and was never reconstructed. The lake had been called Olive Lake and, I learned, the stream there was still called Olive Creek.

Upon my arrival at Wray, I met a young man who was interested in local history. His name was Leo McCoy. He soon introduced me to several elderly men on the street. None knew anything of the Olives from Texas. However, when I asked one of these old gentlemen as to the location of Olive Lake, he replied, "Why it's right out there in H4 Draw." At the mention of this old road brand of the Olives of 1876, H4, my ears stood up. And it proved to be the mention of this enduring old cattle brand that convinced me that the lake and stream had actually been named after the Olives. And added proof was soon forthcoming.

In Wray, we visited with Cal Webster at his home. Mr. Webster was then ninety-two years old. He had ridden for the Three Bars, the old American Cattle Company and had arrived in the area in 1884, he said. The folklore was rich with stories of the Olive brothers at that time, he recalled. But as he related some of the stories they proved to be events that had happened *after* Print Olive and his brothers had left the North Fork range. Mr. Webster called the area of Olive Creek "H4 Draw." He stated positively that it was the headquarters region of the Olive cow camp. He spoke of Olive as "O. P." Olive.

On a farm west of Wray we talked with another genuine old-time cowboy, Bill Toner. He was hard of hearing, but sharp and perceptive. Toner told of the old ranches of the North Fork country, calling many ranchers by their given names. He told tales of the far-off Montana cattle range where he had worked as a young man and to which he had trailed cattle. The area in question had always been H4 Draw, he said. He told of a great farewell party the Olives had given when they left the range, inviting ranchers from near and far to bring all their womenfolk and attend a two-day dance in celebration of their move to Nebraska range.

H4 Draw is itself an unspectacular draw leading down from the hills south to the North Fork steam. Several fine springs form its headwaters. The water is clear and pure and flows constantly, winter or summer. It lies on the south side of U.S. Highway 34, just east of the town of Wray, Colorado.[8] It was the damming of this small stream, called Olive Creek, to make a watering place for their cattle that later led to the erection of a substantial dam for recreational purposes.[9]

The town of Wray, so the Colorado history books tell us, was named after "John Wray, an Olive foreman." This information was credited to Sheriff Lovell of Yuma County in *Colorado Magazine* 20 no. 3 (May 1943): 117. This error was copied from an earlier issue of that magazine, September 1932, p. 183, and is an example of how original error gains prestige if it is allowed to exist and be repeated without questioning. For when the writer inquired into the naming of the town it was discovered that an older brother, James Thomas (Tom) Wray was the man for whom the town was actually named.[10] It was this man, Tom Wray, who guided the Olive H4 herd into the Republican Valley in 1876 and up "Rock Creek Fork," as it was then called, to Corral Canyon and, later still, to H4 Draw on little Olive Creek. The Tom Wray mentioned stayed on at Olive Creek and operated a horse ranch after the Olives withdrew from the range. With his younger brother, John Wray, he also operated a cow ranch on Stinking Water Creek in Nebraska. Both brothers were top cowmen, highly respected, and have now been dead for more than forty years.

Before leaving H4 Draw, Print Olive dispatched his brother Bob and their top bronc rider, "Nigger Jim" Kelly, on an exploration trip into the central and western Nebraska range country. The two brought back a favorable report on the Dismal and Loup River ranges. The Olive brothers then moved five big herds, consisting of about 15,000 head of Texas longhorn cattle, on to the range east from the North and Cody claimings at the head of the Dismal River's south fork. From there eastward to the Dismal confluence with the Middle Loup, the Olive brothers claimed range in 1877–78. This area is still a fine cattle country as well as also now supporting, between the two streams, the Nebraska National Forest Preserve (Bessey Division), first planted in the year 1910. Seedlings from this sandhills forest are now planted all over the United States.

Had the Olive brothers remained on either the North Fork (Colorado) range or the Dismal (Nebraska) range they would have fared better. But Print Olive was an ambitious man who thought and planned big. As the recognized head of his clan he must plan for all families and family members. So he looked for wider and better range, where their individual and collective interests could be expanded.

Print's trips to Kearney, Nebraska—supply point on the main line of the Union Pacific—took him across a great buffalo grass pasture called the Muddy Creek country. Here the buffalo grass stood five inches in height and the bluestem in the valleys grew wither-high to their saddle horses. It was yet an unorganized county when he first saw it, but it was called "Kountze County," after the famous banking houses of that name at Omaha and Denver who made many cattle loans in the area. Later it was named Custer County, after Bvt. Gen. George Armstrong Custer.

The Olives soon moved their ranch headquarters to a school section on the South Loup River. About fifty miles south from there, at Plum Creek (now Lexington) on the main line of the Union Pacific, they built homes for their wives and families. They moved several thousand head of their cattle down on to the Custer County range, out of the Sand Hills. They now had approximately 25,000 head of cattle on the central Nebraska range.[11]

This latter move proved to be a mistake. The rich, black land of Custer County, unlike the sandy hills to the west, was inviting thousands of settlers. Most of the newcomers were poor, often propertyless. They came with determination to gain possession of some of the black land. Most of them were honest, hard working, and with a sense of integrity. The writer's grandparents on both sides were among these pioneer settlers and cattlemen who came at this time to the new land.[12]

But not all were honest. Soon a few were slaughtering range cattle, selling the beef in Kearney markets as "slow elk." Among these thieves and first-class suspects were Manley Caple, eventually hung as a horse thief; a man named Christiansen from Sweetwater, whose jaw Print Olive broke for stealing his cattle; Ami W. Ketchum, a young horseshoer who led a nest of thieves on Clear Creek; and Luther Mitchell, an older man with whom Ketchum lived.[13]

Print and the other cowmen had talked over their troubles and Print became, as the historian Butcher told it "the prime mover in an attempt to drive the cattle thieves from the country." Print had been elected president of the Cattle Grower's Association in Custer County at that time.

When Print elected to move against the rustlers he had Sheriff Anderson of Buffalo County deputize Bob Olive so he could arrest Ketchum and bring him to trial.[14] Manley Caple, already in the toils of the law, had implicated Ketchum with his cattle theft. At the Mitchell homestead where Bob went to arrest Ketchum he was killed by old man Mitchell and the young horseshoer. The murderers fled the country. When they were returned by the sheriff of Keith County, Print paid $700 reward for the two, took them up the nearest canyon, and promptly hung them. Two of the hanging party, a saloonkeeper and the hotelman from Plum Creek, returning to town past the bodies that night, poured the remains of their whiskey jug over the heads of the hanged men and touched them off with a match.[15] Print Olive, at the ranch at this time and in no way responsible for the burning and mutilation of the bodies, had his name forever linked with this act of pyromania on the part of the dissolute townsmen.

Tried for the murder, though freed of the charges of burning the bodies, Print was found guilty and sentenced to life in the penitentiary. He was freed in twenty months when the Supreme Court of Nebraska found that he was tried in a court in Adams County, Nebraska, having no jurisdiction over the case.[16] He returned to his ranch on the South Loup to face the great blizzards that raged over the Nebraska range that winter of 1880–81. The heavy losses on the range caused him to decide on a move southward. Ira Olive remained to become a banker and successful rancher, but Print turned his frozen-tailed cow herd south along the old Texas cattle trail, not stopping until he found good range on the Smoky Hill River in Kansas. There he became a successful cattleman again, a director in the West Central Kansas Cattle Growers Association. He purchased forty acres of land adjoining Dodge City and there built a fine home for his wife and family. His four boys attended Boot Hill school. His wife became active in Dodge City social and church life.[17]

Print Olive was always an active man. Now he entered into one of the most productive periods of his life. In addition to the Smoky Hill ranch he developed a fine ranch on the Sawlog, twelve miles north of Dodge. Later, he established a good horse ranch in Lane County. He bought property south of Dodge, across the river on the Jones and Plummer Trail. He opened a large meat market in Dodge City, an outlet for his beef. He traded in cattle and horses, bringing many more thousands up the Texas trail. He prospered and associated with other cattlemen such as Martin Culver, H. M. Beverly, Chalkley Beeson, Robert M. Wright, A. H. McCoy, Hi Kollar, W. I. Harwood, George Reighard, R. J. Hardesty, Sim Holstein, and others. Both the *Kansas Cowboy*, published at Sidney and the *Globe-Livestock Journal*, published at Dodge, mentioned him frequently in their columns, and his visits to Garden City, Sidney, Dodge City, and other points were recorded. He was referred to as "one of our most sagacious livestock men."

When the blizzards of the winter of 1885–86 struck, Print and his sons were riding the range, trying to save their cattle. They drove in what they could and skinned the rest. Print had erected enormous cattle sheds for protection, but the snows and wind came so quickly the stricken animals failed to reach the shelters.

Then came the late spring of 1886, wet, cold, stormy. The weakened animals that lived now died by the thousands along the drift fence of the Smoky Hill Cattle Pool. Dead cattle covered the plains from the Smoky Hill to the Arkansas, and the icy waters of that stream were choked with countless emaciated and mummified carcasses. Looking down from his saddle upon his dead cattle, Print realized the end had come for wintering cattle on the open range. He had been looking elsewhere for other business interests and was now pleased that he had been one of the first to back Martin Culver, H. P. Myton, and W. S. Smith in the boom town Culver was building just across the Colorado state line, on the Atchison, Topeka, and Santa Fe Railroad. "Trail City," they had named it, in Bent County, Colorado, S17–Twp S33–Range 41. The names of Martin Culver, H. P. Myton, and W. S. Smith appeared on the certificate of incorporation, dated 5 November, 1885. Capital stock of $20,000 was divided into 200 shares of $100.00 each by the Trail City Town and Improvement Co. Incorporated in Kansas, Finney County (Garden City).

That previous summer Print had engaged workers to erect a large stable and wagon yard on a double lot he had purchased on Trail City's main street. He named it the "Trail's End." He built another good frame saloon building next door to the general store operated by his friend, H. M. Beverly, who had also served as a lieutenant in the Confederate army during the war and was a close friend. A few blocks northwest he erected a small frame building for a home for himself and his negro man, Sam, who worked at the barn. A partner, Haynes, operated the saloon. Now Print turned the skinning of the dead cattle over to his son, Billy, and he headed westward to Trail City.

"Trail," as the cattlemen called it, was a town boomer's mistake from the start. The National Cattle Trail, which it was designed to serve, failed to get congressional support and died.[18] The season of 1885 had been fair; 1886 promised to be better. But already, settlers were attempting to fence off parts of the trail. Within three or four months, Print realized that the boom had ended, and he found a buyer for his Trail City enterprises. It was his desire to get back to the Sawlog ranch, tighten up his operations, and pay off some debts he owed relatives in Texas and the bank. The first week in August the businesses were sold, the new operators to take over on the fifteenth of the month.

The night of the fifteenth, Print and the new owners celebrated the deal with a friendly poker game and drinks at his old saloon. Late that night, about midnight, he walked down to the stable to talk to Sam Johnson, his black helper. At the barn he met Joe Sparrow, a young man whom he had hired for a trail trip a few years before at Goliad, Texas. Sparrow was now twenty-seven years old, a big man, standing six feet two inches, and very handsome.

Joe Sparrow was almost the antithesis of Print Olive. Joe was big; Print was small. Joe was slow moving; Print moved quickly, like a cat. Joe was slow in speech; Print spoke quickly, with decision. These differences had come between the two men on the cattle trail, and Print had been glad to pay off the big cowboy at Dodge City. Later, Sparrow ran cattle in the Indian Territory. Once, in wintertime, he came to Print and borrowed a hundred dollars to pay off his cowboys who were riding for him. He had managed to pay it all back but an important ten dollars. This amount he owed Print for many months and did not act as if he intended to repay the loan. Added to this amount was a small feed bill that he had run up at the Olive barn in Trail City. Although Print had never been a man to press a debtor for money, he knew the reputation as a deadbeat Joe Sparrow had earned among the cattlemen. Now he asked Sparrow to repay the loan and the feed bill on Sparrow's horse. Sparrow hemmed and hawed and gave Print no satisfaction.

With Sparrow at this discussion between the two men was a man named John Stansfield, a county officer from Hamilton County, Kansas, who frequently came up to Trail City for a binge. As Print and Sparrow quarreled over the money, Stansfield took up Sparrow's quarrel. Print warned Stansfield to stay out of the argument. He had had Stansfield ejected from his saloon a few days previously and now mentioned this to Stansfield. The three men eventually parted, but not without Print giving Sparrow a warning to have the money by afternoon, the following day, when Print expected to leave town, "or one of us will leave Trail in a box."

Since all three men had been drinking, those who heard the quarrel, including "Nigger Sam," Johnson thought the trouble would be over, once the men had slept on it. Print went straight from the barn to his house where he went to bed. As Sparrow and Stansfield left the barn, following the chewing Print had given Sparrow, John Stansfield was heard to remark, "You shoot the son-of-a-bitch, Joe, and I'll back you up."[19]

Print arose late the following morning. He packed his things at the house, since he would take the evening train to Dodge City. He left orders with Sam to carry his things down to the hotel where Murph Ward's hack would pick them up and take them to Coolidge, Kansas, where he would board the train. Then he started down to the saloon to have a final word with Walt Hart who was tending bar. It was midafternoon, a hot, August day with a south wind whipping clouds of talcum-dry dust up the main street.[20]

Within the saloon, Sparrow and Stansfield had stationed themselves before the bar and near a window where they could watch Print Olive's approach from the street. Walt Hart was busy at the back bar, cleaning a ledge. Although there was a man digging a pit or well near the open back door, there were no others inside the saloon.

As Print stepped up the limestone steps to the doorway of the building, Sparrow fondled, then drew his 44 revolver. Print was wiping the sweat and dust from his brow with a red bandana as he stepped into the building. He was in his shirt-sheeves, completely unarmed. Before a word was spoken, Sparrow aimed his revolver and fired. The bullet struck Print in the breast. He cried out in pain and surprise, "My God, Joe, don't murder me!"

Joe Sparrow fired a second shot, the bullet again striking the doomed man in the breast. Print fell heavily back against the door casing, his head striking the limestone slab as he fell to the floor. Sparrow now stepped in closer, leaned over, holding the big revolver within three feet of the dying man's head. He carefully aimed and pulled the trigger, sending the bullet into Print Olive's brain.

The entire murder, so well had Sparrow planned it, took only a few seconds. Walter Hart jumped from behind the bar, seized Sparrow's revolver. Sparrow leaped over the prostrate form of the dead man and ran into the street where he was soon captured by the town marshal.[21] Stansfield fled out the back door and escaped, never to be heard of again.[22]

So ended the life of Prentice Olive, Texas cowman. His career had spanned an era, that of the range cattle industry—1840 to 1886. It was a career that not only ran contemporaneously with the era but, one might say, symbolized the age itself. For there was the fierce vigor and drive of Print Olive's life, similar to and in harmony with the activity of that period of history. There was grave lawlessness on the part of men, there was the lust for living, and the enormous expenditures of energy devoted to creating and building new things. There was the drive for accomplishment, married to the faculty for improvisation that made a winning team. And contemporary with the visible rawness and crudeness that shone out like a beacon in both the man and his era, there was a tenderness that cropped out onto the surface from beneath. It was the feeling all good men had for the really vital things they cherished and contended for—the love and respect of their womenfolk and the desire to create a better life for their children. And Print Olive had a good wife to whom he was devoted. As the frontier encompassed all these things, so did Prentice Olive's life reflect them back as from a mirror of that time.

The type of man Olive appeared to be, by those who knew him best, is shown in the commemorative testimonial written about him by brothers of Corona Lodge, I.O.O.F., Dodge City, Kansas, the men who buried him. Within a few paragraphs of this document reposes greater truth about him than the millions of words written about him in the last three-quarters of a century.[23]

Olive's footsteps were felt at other points in Colorado, no doubt, since he was an active cattleman, buying, selling, dealing. But his presence in the state left little mark upon Colorado, or even upon the industry to which he had devoted his life. Still, the name Olive is perpetuated in the Colorado history books that deal with the area around Wray, Colorado, as well as in the many stories and the folklore surrounding old Trail City. And the "Olive decollete holsters," hanging in the many western museums are a reminder of "the Olive Gun Outfit."

Old "Trail" is, today, just a weed-grown and glass-littered ten-acre patch south of Highway 50, on the state line between the highway and the Santa Fe tracks. Tourists, fleeing westward from the "over-commercialized" places at Dodge City, Abilene, and Wichita and other "cow-towns" to the east, now flash by the site of Trail City at eighty and ninety miles per hour. They are searching the west for unsullied points of historical interest, though scarcely one in a hundred thousand has learned where to look for such sites as old Trail City, in Colorado.

As I stood at that old spot one evening, a meadowlark was singing near the limestone ruins of the old hotel that had stood near a giant cottonwood tree. I felt myself fairly surrounded by the Muse of History. Through my mind's ears I heard the bawling of the longhorns as the point of a herd swung up the main street at Trail City, the tin cans tied to the ends of the cowboys' lariats rattling and clanging in rude accompaniment to their shrill cries. Under the clouds of dust raised by twelve thousand hooves, I watched in my mind's eye as their great horned heads swung by on their way to the Yellowstone. And I contemplated the rich, adventurous lives of such Texas boys as Prentice Olive, many of whom came to their trail's end in just such a manner as did he. At that moment I came to regard the violent deaths suffered by such men not as just "western reading material" but as great western tragedies. For when a man dies by the act of violence on the part of another man, murder has been committed. When a widow is left, as was Mrs. Prentice Olive, with a family of small children to rear alone, young teenage boys who needed a father's guidance, and without a substantial estate to soften the blow of her husband's death, then a great wrong has been inflicted upon both her and her family and society. And when you have seen the suffering of even later generations from such an historical act of ugliness and anger, then you realize what an evil act has been done.

Nearly every death scene that took place on the frontier, resulting from such an act of violence, was a tragedy to some wife, mother, father, or relative. In my research on the life of Prentice Olive I found descendants sharing the remorse for Joe Sparrow's thoughtless deed as well as the stigma of living under the legend provided by the many "western" writers who have recorded the uglier phases of his life. While it is true, as Frank Dobie has pointed out, that we cannot deal with the frontier period without recognizing its violence, still, as earnest scribes, and as astute recorders of our past, we should at all times attempt to place such violence as we must deal with in its proper historical perspective. For there is an important lesson to be learned, and to be taught, from the violence itself, a lesson so old and well recognized that it has appeared in the earliest writings of humanity, usually in some such form as "Thou shalt not kill." Although callous commercial writers will continue to fill TV screens, motion picture films, books, magazines, and newspapers with their diet of western crime, sin, murder, rape, sadism, and flagellations, we Westerners should pause and reflect. Let them have it. Let us learn from the deaths of men such as Prentice Olive to record death just as it occurred, to make no attempt to profit from such tragedy any more than we would try to profit from war. Let us report accurately, not alter facts and color the story to fit what, in our minds, may be the desires, specifications, and formulas of pandering literary buyers. I have the faith that "truth will out." The quicker the better. And since truth is always stranger—and more readable—than fiction, I feel that honest western material, properly researched and well written, will always find a responsible and receptive American market.

Notes

1. All news stories, court records and sources of the time agree on this.

2. Published articles and stories that repeat these old falsehoods are:

The Saturday Evening Post, Mari Sandoz, "Tyrant of the Plains," June 7, 1958.

Cavalier Magazine, Lewis Nordyke, "Man Burner From Texas," March 1959.

Fury Magazine, L. Gordon Jacot, "The Mad Outlaw," September 1960.

True, The Man's Magazine, John Feack, "One Man Mafia of the Plains," September 1960.

Real West, James L. Carter, "Who Killed Print Olive?" March 1960.

Frontier Times, Van W. Tilford, "Print Olive," Winter 1960 issue.

True Frontier, Fred Huston, "Man Burner From Texas," Summer 1974.

Great West, Budington Swanson, "Death At Devils Gap," August 1973.

3. Scores of men and women who knew the Olive families personally spoke highly of them as "all good people," and "I liked both Print and Ira" and "they were most friendly men." Nearly a hundred men agreed to testify for Prentice Olive at his Nebraska trial.

4. The old photo of "I. P. Olive" in Solomon Devoe Butcher's *Pioneer History of Custer County, Nebraska* (The Merchants Publishing Co., Denver, Colorado, 1901) bears small resemblance to the real I. P. Olive. Al Olive, Print Olive's son, rejected it as the image of his father, gave the author a genuine photo. We must assume that Butcher, an honest chronicler, was

given a false photo, twenty years after Olive left Nebraska. This false photo has been retouched and used many times to illustrate Olive stories, and is even today recognized as genuine by some members of the Nebraska Historical Society.

5. See Leo McCoy's *Map of Cattle Range on North Fork, Colorado,* in author's files on Olive families.

6. The factual account of these killings has never been told before, though James Olive hinted of them as reported in Butcher's *History.* The story is told in detail in a book on I. P. Olive's life, the material coming from various members of the Olive family. See Harry E. Chrisman, *Ladder of Rivers* (Athens, Ohio: Swallow Press, 1961).

7. Corral Canyon lies about halfway between Haigler and Parks, Nebraska, on the south side of U.S. Highway 34.

8. This is SE1/4; sec. 5; twp. 1; N1/4; R43 W, Yuma County, Colorado.

9. Fred Count owned this land in 1958.

10. See "Letters" in author's Olive file from Mrs. Clara Wray, Culbertson, Nebraska, widow of John Wray. From Mary Wray Darwell, McCook, Nebraska, and Mrs. Frank Leu, North Platte, Nebraska, daughters of James Thomas (Tom) Wray. Also see original source of Lovell's remark in *History of the State of Colorado* (Chicago: Blakely Co., 1889), p. 355 by Frank Hall, for Rocky Mountain Historical Company.

11. Frank H. Young, Custer County clerk, estimated for tax purposes about 1879–80 that the Olive brothers had 31,271 head of cattle on the Custer County, Nebraska, range. See Young's "Notebook," in possession of Mr. and Mrs. Wayne Jenkins. Jenkins Ranch, Oconto, Nebraska.

12. Butcher's *Pioneer History of Custer County, Nebraska;* see Joseph M. Chrisman, cattleman, and Carlyle Hunter, deputy sheriff, who came to the area in 1881 and 1878, respectively.

13. These four men are cited in most histories: (in addition to Butcher's *History*):

Trail of the Loup, H. W. Fought and W. W. Haskell, 1906, N. P.

History of the State of Nebraska, A. T. Andreas, Western Historical Co., Chicago, 1882.

Olive's Last Roundup, A. O. Jenkins, Sherman County *Nebraska Times,* Loup City, Nebraska, 1928.

Book of Facts, George E. Benschoter, Loup City, Nebraska.

52

14. Bob Olive (wanted by the Texas Rangers for the murders of several rustlers in Texas) went by the name of Bob Stevens in Nebraska.

15. This is the Olive side of the story, told by Al Olive. Also see Butcher's *History*, p. 51.

16. Nebraska *Supreme Court Records*, Book 1.

17. Now NW Dodge City—W1/2; SW 1/4; sec. 26; twp. 26; R–25; still known as "Olive's Addition."

18. Congress failed to approve the National Cattle Trail; settlers moved in and fenced the lands, beef prices dropped, the blizzards of 1885–86 struck. Everything conspired to kill the range cattle and trail driving industries.

19. Al Olive, Print Olive's son, attended three trials with his mother. He told the author of his father's Trail City enterprises. "Nigger Sam" Johnson had related much to Al in later years. Also see Court Records, Pueblo, Colorado.

20. Al Olive said that Joe Sparrow knew that his father was leaving Trail City for good that evening, and laid for him when he knew his father was unarmed "and would least expect an attack." When asked what sort of a man Sparrow was, if he was an "outlaw or a desperado," Al Olive snorted. "He was nothing; just *nothing!*"

21. Sparrow was tried and convicted, won a new trial, but the jury was hung up. Tried the third time, the jury freed him.

22. Perhaps the most outrageous report of the murder, not even excluding Miss Sandoz's rendition in her book *The Cattlemen* (Hastings House Publishers, N.Y. 1958), is that filed with the Colorado Historical Society as "Along The Cattle Trail," Hamer Norris, Document no. 43, a collection of interviews by Civil Works Administration workers, pp. 187–88 (Pamphlet No. 355, Doc. 1–53 and Pamphlet 355, Doc. 54–63, Prowers and Clear Creek Counties, Colorado). Also see *Lamar* (Colo.) *Register*, 7 March, 1928.

23. Print was memorialized, the Lodge stating that:

> He was a man and a brother with qualities of head and heart
> which we all admired . . . that he has shown himself at all times
> to be a very worthy brother and member of our Order . . . we
> cheerfully record his many virtues and finer qualities . . . that
> we mourn for him as an unfortunate brother with loving wife

53

and children, whose pangs of sadness and sorrow are more
deeply felt than by all others and to whom he has been a kind
and affectionate husband and father . . . and we hereby extend
our deepest sympathy . . . and spread upon our lodge records this
Memorial and extend it to the city papers to be published. . . .

Just the previous year, Print had been elected to serve on the Reception
Committee of the Cattlemen's Convention with Martin Culver, Col. R. J.
Hardesty, and Robert M. Wright.

6

The Devil's Cattle Trap

Nature, in a cantankerous mood, brought havoc to the ranchers of western Nebraska.

Not many people have heard of The Devil's Cattle Trap. The area is off the main traveled highways, and folks who live within ten miles of the place today wouldn't recognize it by that name. But there was a time, back in the 1870s, when the area referred to by that name conveyed a sinister meaning to the neighboring ranchers. Those deadly traps are still set today, ready to be sprung on any unfortunate creature, human or beast, that wanders unknowingly into that area.

The first story I heard of the cattle traps concerned a Texas cowboy, Barney McGee, and a pal named Cornet.

McGee was a carefree young man who came north with a Mabry and Bunton herd from the Goliad country in the late 1870s. He stayed north and worked for Creighton's; later he went with Sturgis and Lane on the Bridle Bit ranch, and later still, he worked for the Hart outfit in the western end of the Nebraska panhandle.

The Hart ranch produced fine colts from a small herd of brood mares they kept, some of which were of Steel Dust breeding and had been bought from the Olive brothers in Texas. These colts were greatly in demand as three-year-olds, and the geldings were sold to other ranches to be broken out for fine cutting and roping horses.

One spring in the late 1870s, the Hart outfit sold to Carey, in Wyoming, twelve head of these better colts. They were to be delivered to the Carey camp on Horse Creek, just across the state line in Wyoming. Barney McGee and his friend Cornet were to make the delivery.

There had been much concern about cattle rustlers and horse thieves on the vast Panhandle range, and the Hart ranch, Brown's ranch, Sturgis and Lane and other cattlemen had lost quite a few head of livestock in those years. The Hart foreman had given his men orders to shoot on sight any man caught burning a brand on a range calf.

The Bridle Bit foreman had chewed his red mustache until it was as ragged as his cowboys' shirt-tails, but no rustlers had been turned up. No trails of livestock that had been driven from the range were ever uncovered, but the losses continued to mystify the ranchers.

As McGee and Cornet set out with their little band of colts, accompanied by an old pack mare, they little realized that their journey would solve the problem of rustling on that range.

Late in the morning as the cowboys jogged along with their colts, McGee riding in the lead and Cornet following along behind, a few of the colts broke away and headed toward a greasewood-covered area where some rather unusual hummocks of earth dotted the landscape. Among these mounds of cracked clay ran wild animal trails, and good grass was to be found in patches. The colts headed directly toward a nearby spring, paying no attention to the hummocks over which they clambered, smelling only the water. As McGee turned back to help Cornet drive the colts to the trail, he saw that two or three of them were becoming bogged atop the hummocks. By the time he and his friend had chased out all the colts that could travel, and driven them a quarter of a mile from the boggy spring area, they were aware that a half dozen of the colts were bogged fast on the separate knolls, or "boils," as they appeared to be. Riding back to one of the hummocks to inspect it, McGee's gelding stepped squarely into the oily clay mud at the center of the mound and quickly sank in above the knees. Acting instantly, McGee spurred his horse out of the quagmire, but not without considerable trouble, for the mud, though soft as a toasted marshmallow, had the consistency of a good quality of glue.

The sides of the hummocks were a dark gray, and the boys soon found that while they could ride their horses along the slopes, where the crumpled clay had dried as hard as rock, once a hoof touched the *center* of the boil the animal would start sinking as if in a quicksand. The frightened colts that were now mired in the cattle traps were plunging and screaming, some of them enveloped almost up the withers, their nostrils distended and the whites of their eyes showing their terror.

Both McGee and Cornet were aware of the danger to the colts, and each hurriedly took down his lariat and attempted to pull a colt from the bog. But it was no use, and it was quickly apparent that the oily clay that held them was a different matter than the black river mud or the shifting quicksands along the banks of the North Platte River. Seeing that it would take both saddle horses to pull one colt from the sticky clay, McGee and Cornet joined forces, each putting a loop on the same colt and exerting a steady pull that slowly freed the animal from the bog, although the strain on its throat threatened to pull the neck down and ruin the animal forever as a saddle horse. But in this manner the two boys eventually freed the six trapped colts, drove them in with the rest of the herd and again started down the trail to the Carey horse camp, but with all of the colts plastered with gummy clay from the bogs.

Within a half hour, traveling in the hot sun, Cornet realized that their troubles were just beginning. The six head that had been bogged, together with the pack mare which had also encased her front legs in the sticky mud, now lagged at the rear of the band, for the oily alkali clay had begun to form a coating like a plaster cast on the animals. As a piece of the cast would pull loose as a result of the animals' movement, both hair and some flesh would come off with it. Cornet, alarmed, signaled a halt and the two cowboys debated a course of action. They decided to push on to Horse Creek, a few miles ahead, for the night.

They reached the creek late in the evening, still twenty miles from the Carey horse camp. They quickly hobbled the colts that had not become encased in the clay, pulled off their saddles and washed the clay from their mounts and the pack mare, using their saddle blankets to scrape away the caked mud, once it had been somewhat softened by liberal applications of creek water. Then they lay down beneath some cottonwood trees for the night. But McGee found sleep elusive, and lay staring at the stars, contemplating the task of cleaning up the colts that lay ahead of them. He knew the Carey foreman would never receive the animals in the condition they were in, encased in hard casts of oily clay from the bogs.

At daybreak the two boys arose. They gathered the stray colts and began the process of heeling and throwing them, one by one, and to soaking up and washing off the baked clay. Carrying water in their hats to the colts was too slow a method, so they soon began to throw and hog-tie the colts in the shallow water.

It was a tedious and laborious work, for the water was cold and did little more than permit them to tear away the hard clay, frequently taking some hide and hair with it.

"These colts will look like buffalo calves shedding off, come spring," McGee muttered as he rubbed on the mass with his saddle blanket.

The two cowboys labored all that day on the creek bank, cleaning four of the worst cases and freeing the colts of their earthen caskets. That night they slept little, in spite of their weariness. Their food had run out, and men sleep poorly on empty stomachs.

The following morning they cleaned up the two remaining colts, then spent more time washing away the clay from the eyes and nostrils of some of the worse sufferers. Late that morning they left the creek for the Carey camp. That afternoon they met a cowboy from the PF ranch who shared with them a can of tomatoes and some stale bread he had wrapped in his slicker. Late in the evening they arrived at the Carey horse camp, where they related their experience to the Carey wranglers.

The strange story of the Devil's Cattle Trap spread over the entire range and was soon known to all the cattlemen in that area. "Cattle losses" which had formerly been attributed to rustlers were now properly blamed on the boggy cattle traps which claimed many of the cattle that wandered down to the greasewood springs to drink and fell into their grip. The mute testimony of bleached cattle and horse skulls, and the whitened bones that worked their way to the tops of the mounds from the bogs below, was proof enough that human thieves were not to blame for the losses.

In 1881, a United States deputy surveyor named George W. Fairfield passed that way on business and made a careful study of the boggy area. In his field notebook he told about the dangerous bogs, titling his work "The Devil's Cattle Trap." That article remains available today in the vault of the State Board of Educational Lands and Funds Office in Nebraska. In the office of the surveyor general, Plattsmouth, Nebraska, is a map which was also filed by Fairfield on 10 April 1882. The map shows in detail the area where the cowboys, McGee and Cornet, fought their life-and-death struggle with the bogs for the lives of their employer's colts several years before. On the map is a notation showing that the area was first surveyed in 1880 by a Robert Harvey, who himself almost fell victim to the bogs.

On his recollection of the bog area, surveyor Fairfield wrote:

> It has the appearance of an artistically laid out land-scape, freshly dug up. There are mounds in all sorts of fantastic shapes and the appearance of paths and walks laid out in every direction through and among the mounds.
>
> The crust on the sides of the mounds is as hard as stone and perfectly firm and strong enough to bear up under a large horse or ox. But it is so thin and soft on top that a pound weight laid on it will sink at once into a sticky solution of chalk, or something of the consistency of cream, and so deep that I could not find bottom with a pole 15-feet long.
>
> Any beast that walks on top of the mounds is doomed and will speedily sink out of sight. The ranchmen say there are hundreds of cattle lost there every year and they are going to put a good barbed wire fence around the whole place.
>
> I have the honor to submit that the name of this place should be *The Devil's Cattle Trap.*

Surveyor Fairfield went on to tell of a mule that was with him and his party that became covered with the plaster cast afforded by the bogs. "When that mule got dry, there was a hard crust almost as white as snow on him, and we had to wash him three times with warm water and soap before we could get him perfectly clean."

After reading Fairfield's statement about the mule, one can understand the problem that confronted McGee and his friend Cornet, when they were attempting to clean up their colts with only cold creek water, saddle blankets, and their bare hands.

The writer first learned of these bogs when crossing that country south of present Lyman, Nebraska, with a U.S. government line crew in 1923. When the Gering Valley irrigation project was undertaken, and a tunnel driven beneath the range of hills to the west of present Scott's Bluff National Monument, we constructed power lines ahead of heavy ditching equipment (draglines), dismantling the power lines when the ditches had been completed. One lineman with our crew, a good friend and a top-notch man in all respects, was lanky Homer Williams. Homer was an older man and one of wide experience who, among other things, had done some cowboying in his youth.

As we neared the site of the Devil's Cattle Trap with our line work, Homer began relating weird tales he had heard from the cowboys about this region. He told us of McGee and Cornet, a tale he had heard from the foreman of the old PF ranch on the North Platte River, near the Wyoming-Nebraska state line. As Homer described the bogs, telling us of their danger to people and beast alike, some of the men grew skeptical. But one morning Shorty Bannon, our foreman, permitted eight of us to ride the big Mack truck into that area for a "look-see." That was the time we all decided we wanted no part of constructing a high line across those hummocks!

On all sides, as we entered the area, we could see from our high position on the truck scores of mud pots and mounds, or "boils," just as Fairfield had described them. The sides of the hummocks were littered with the bleached bones of former victims. At the center of each mound we could see where the bones had been regurgitated. On the slopes, the boggy stuff was dry and of a much different consistency than the creamy center. We all dismounted from the truck and walked cautiously among the mounds, with Homer's dire warning to stay away from the center of the mounds ringing in our ears.

Homer grasped a pike-pole from the side of the truck and he and I climbed up one of the nearby mounds, carefully testing the ground as we went. The twelve-foot pike-pole was one used by the groundmen to support the big power poles erectly in their holes as the earth was tamped in firmly around them. Stepping to the edge of a boil, Homer placed the pole's spiked end into the mud and held the pike erect, while letting it sink slowly into the bog. The pike-pole went down, down, down into the mud. When only a foot of the pole remained above the bog, I stepped to the opposite side of the hole and with the tip of a finger pushed the remainder of the pole into the goo. That long pole never reached bottom! And then to our delight as we stepped back to watch it, the pole began to slowly rise from the bog, not stopping until almost three-quarters of its length was again clear of the spongy surface.

A few years ago, while revisiting in that areaa, I thought I would see if Homer Williams was still there for I had heard he lived nearby. We stopped at a house where a dinner party was in progress one Sunday afternoon. When I inquired at the door about Homer, a young woman in the group said, "I'm sorry but Homer Williams is dead. But I am his daughter. Can I help you?"

After a friendly visit, during which I recounted our story of visiting the bogs, and had secured the names of some farmers who would again join me in a visit to those natural boils, we departed.

At the home of Fred Banta, six miles south of Lyman, Nebraska, we paid a visit to three of the mounds on his property. Banta spoke of the bogs as "Witches' Bogs," which residents of the area call them today. On the slope of one of the boils, I looked down at the spongy area at its center, about three feet in diameter. Nothing appeared to have changed in the thirty years since I had last seen the cattle traps. Taking a nearby seven-foot corner fence post, I pushed it down into the center. Like the pike-pole Homer and I had shoved into the bog years before, the post disappeared from sight, only to make a gradual reappearance. We were told by Banta that a post set into the mud and left there would work up in the fall months, but that it would sink down again in the spring!

A John Deere tractor was once accidentally bogged in one of the nearby traps, Banta related. The next day it had disappeared forever! He also told of a Cheyenne hunter, an elderly man about seventy years old who came in the fall of 1961 to hunt pheasants in that section. This man inadvertently stepped into one of the bogs, and almost before he realized what had happened was in it up to the waist.

Fortunately for him, someone had been using a splintered half of a tongue from a farm wagon to test the depth of that particular bog, and the long stick of wood was within the old man's reach. Using it, the hunter was able, after a long struggle, to extricate himself and save his life. He came to the farmhouse covered with the sticky plaster, and the family realized at once what had happened and helped him clean up.

The experience had exhausted and angered him, and though he was hunting on posted land, he chided the farmer for not fencing the boggy area and placing Keep Out signs on each mound!

Some years ago John Brammeier, then three years old, walked into one of the bogs near his father's farmhouse. His grandmother heard the child crying, rushed out, and managed to pull him free, though he was in up to the armpits.

One of Banta's cows once became bogged on a Sunday when the family was away from home. On Monday, when she was discovered, only her head was above the mud. A long chain was quickly worked around her neck and using a tractor, they slowly drew her from the bog. But the animal died from the injuries incurred in her rescue.

More fortunate was a cow R. H. Miller of Scottsbluff, Nebraska, helped rescue from one of the bogs when the Miller family lived in the area from 1910 to 1920. The cow was a fine Guernsey, but a very stubborn animal. When she bogged she would make no effort to free herself, though in up to the stomach. Miller conceived the idea of "helping her to help herself." He collected some dried grass, small sticks, and dried weeds. Placing these at her rear end, he set the brush afire. "She came out of there plenty fast," Miller related afterward.

Almost every farmer in that neighborhood can tell of some experience or misadventure connected with the bogs, yet so far as I could determine no human has ever lost his or her life in one. In winter, the farmers say, the bogs freeze, but they do not freeze over solid, even in the coldest weather. An oily quality in the clay seems to prevent this.

The earth on the sides of the mounds still has a sinking quality when one steps upon it to the center of the bog on top, where the clay is thick and sticky. If one stamps on the ground heavily the entire mass will quiver like an inverted bowlful of jelly. Once visitors have experienced this sensation of the earth shaking beneath their feet— much like an earthquake without sound effects—they will quickly descend from the mound, for it is a terrifying experience to feel that one's feet rest on a thin crust of earth only inches above the gooey mass that lies just below the surface.

There has been no satisfactory explanation given for the phenomenon of the Devil's Cattle Trap. One theory has been advanced that underground water pressure may account for the manner in which the mud works to the surface, bringing up objects previously sucked under. The mud geysers of Yellowstone Park act in a similar manner. But if there is heat below it is far down, for the mud is cool to the touch at the surface of these western Nebraska bogs. In 1936 a well driller went through the cool bog mud with his drill and had to case it out before reaching a flowing well at eighty-five feet. The well was reported to have flowed a gallon every forty seconds, evidence of some pressure below.

The writer took a few pounds of the white mud home with him and showed it to a nephew who does modeling in clay. It was hoped it might be suited to such a purpose. As the mud dried it took on the consistency of putty or modeling clay. But the oily nature of the clay would not permit the reintroduction of water to maintain its workability, and when it was thoroughly dried it became like stone.

No commercial use has ever been found for the mixture, even if it could be taken in sufficient quantities from the pits. A woman interested in cosmetic manufacture once leased the area. She later dropped the lease, apparently finding that a mudpack of the clay acted on the human skin as it did on the hair and hide of McGee's colts!

Today, that region around the Devil's Cattle Trap is a settled farming community with fine homes and highly developed, irrigated lands. But the bog area remains substantially as it has always been— dangerous to beasts and human beings.

It is an area that will still throw fear into the stoutest heart, should one become lost at night and wandering in the wasteland of obnoxious boils, their gaping mouths wide open and prepared to swallow anything that trespasses on their domain.

If you ever decide to pay a visit to the Devil's Cattle Trap or to test its capacity for snaring the unwary, be sure to take a friend and a long pole with you. For you may need the help of both to extricate yourself, lest you become another of its countless victims!

7

The Covered Wagon
Grows Up

Inventive Ed Hancock, Kansas pioneer, gave to our nation the
comforts of the mobile home.

Eleven-year-old Charles Edward Hancock peered out from the seat
beside his father, high on the covered wagon, and watched the beautiful, black, matched team of mares, Kit and Nell, labor with the heavy
load as the little caravan of wagons crossed the verdant prairieland of
Kansas. He was experiencing an adventure which he would never
forget. As they camped each evening, his mother would start a fire in
her heavy kitchen range which occupied a place on his father's wagon
directly behind the seat. With the wagon sheet rolled half-way back
and smoke rising from the stubby stovepipe, she would cook the
evening meal in full view of her family and the men from the other
two wagons. The sourdough biscuits that came from her oven were a
treat for all and the juicy beef roasts a traveler's joy. She cooked on the
range in the wagon in preference to "squatting like a Comanche
squaw" and cooking on a campfire built on the ground.

As Charles took in the activities each day he could not help but
observe how comfortable the gypsy life of traveling in a covered
wagon was. They were en route to a western Kansas claim, and the
wagon, like a house, offered every member of the family food, shelter,
and security.

During the daytime, when the drivers insisted that the three
wagons continue to roll without stopping every hour for the relief of
one or more of the children, the youngsters were obliged to use the
chambers or pails that were made accessible for their convenience.
The beds they made up in the wagons offered much greater comfort

than did the rocky, wind-blown, sandy prairie with its hummocks of yucca roots and an occasional cactus. So Charles and the other children preferred to sleep in the wagons.

As the Hancock family continued west from Missouri to the claim in western Kansas, the covered wagons began to seem just like home to the boy. He would remember this journey as "life in a home on wheels." In fact, this memory was to supply him with the idea that would take his lifetime to develop and execute into a totally new conception of a vehicle for travel whose improvements will perhaps never be exhausted so long as a people desire to travel in greater comfort and style than did their ancestors. For in Charles Edward Hancock's young, but fertile and ingenious mind, had been planted the seed for today's mobile homes that were to follow.

By 1914, Charles was a man of forty-one, married and the father of several children. He was a contractor-carpenter, living at Liberal, Kansas, where, with his partner, John Baughman, a realtor and financier, he had constructed nearly a hundred new homes. Hancock was the builder, the Baughman Company the seller. Within three more years Hancock had constructed more than 140 homes, all built by hand labor, much of it supplied by himself, his wife, Lottie Grace, and his two half-grown daughters, Mildred and Pauline. Even little Merna and Bud, the younger children helped out. Charles Edward, Jr., although too small to work, was observant and eventually became a successful builder in his own right.

These new homes were erected and sold, but greater publicity was needed to introduce other families to home ownership. Charles Edward Hancock then conceived the idea of a "trailer house." For what was more natural than with the passing of the ox-and-horse-drawn era of history, and the advent of the motor-machine age, that a pioneer builder, like himself, would come to grips with the need of the age—a vehicle that could be drawn behind a motor car, much as a covered wagon was drawn across the plains and mountains by oxen or horses when the Old West was settled. By 1914 he had constructed his first "trailer."

By the year 1916, Hancock had constructed two gigantic houses as big as hayracks, mounted on the running gears of used cars he had located at a nearby garage, each with wheels equipped with pneumatic tires. These "houses on wheels" were pulled by his "Apperson 8,"

Jackrabbit, an auto with an enormous engine and the pulling power to meet most requirements placed upon it by the big house trailers. That Christmas season Hancock, who loved children, took all the small-fry of the town and countryside for rides on his "home on wheels." As they toured the streets of the town the children chanted a refrain taught them by Mrs. Hancock and the girls, one of the earliest if not the first of the "singing commercials" heard in the nation:

> Hancock, Hancock, going for a ride,
> Going to see Old Santa Claus
> DOWN IN SUNNYSIDE!

The parade ended at one of the completed residences in Sunnyside Addition, the old John Baughman homestead, where Old Santa Claus passed out the treats.

An idea now began to grow in Charles Edward Hancock's mind that a smaller, more practical "trailer house" could be constructed and used for travel by his own family as well as be adaptable for a hunting or fishing trip by the menfolk. He set to work and within a few weeks created a trailer house that was a little more streamlined and one that had much greater mobility than his first big houses on wheels. His latest model slept twelve people, had its own stove, kitchen facilities, and lavatory. The toilet facilties still stumped him, so he relied on the same chamber and pails as had the pioneers.

That spring he took a trip with his family to the Rocky Mountains. After a leisurely tour across the gently sloping plains east of the Rockies, he came to Manitou Springs, Colorado, and pulled up before the fashionable hotel where his friend and business associate John Baughman and Mrs. Baughman and their young son Bob were vacationing. Together with the other guests they came out to greet him. The hotel people were dumbfounded at the "home on wheels." Everyone exclaimed about the excellent condition of the trailer after the long trip over primitive roads. For there was hardly a mile of surfaced road at that time between Hancock's home in Kansas and Colorado Springs, Colorado.

One guest, deeply impressed by Hancock's invention said to him, "Why man, you have your own hotel—right on wheels!"

A second guest, an eastern man interested only in automobile stocks, spoke up: "It's just a novelty. Nothing will ever come from it!"

Baughman put an arm around Hancock's shoulders and said quietly, "Pay no attention to that fellow. He's the man I swapped a $1,300 automobile for a 10,000-acre Baca County, Colorado, ranch." Baughman chuckled. "He thinks that land is good for nothing except to feed prairie dogs and jackrabbits."

After a delightful vacation that was low in cost because they had their sleeping and cooking facilities right along with them, Hancock and his family returned to Kansas refreshed and happy. The success of the Colorado trip prompted Hancock to write the Apperson Auto Company, at Kokomo, Indiana, early the following spring, offering to bring the trailer and show them how it operated. The company replied that they were not interested in such a vehicle, to be pulled by a car, but that their interest was in some method for reclining the back of the seat in their touring cars to provide a bed for campers! Hancock had long since passed this point in his thinking on the matter and was disappointed that the automobile firm could not visualize the practicability of the house trailer. However, he agreed to see them. He decided to take his trailer along to live in and cut expense on the way east. Early that year he started for Kokomo, but he never got out of Kansas. A severe snow storm clogged the rutted roads and he was forced to turn back at Dodge City.

In 1917, with the First World War in progress, Hancock's many duties and interests prevented further exploration of the trailer for commercial exploitation. Yet he improved his personal house trailer and made new comfort additions for the family's use. When the war was over, the Hancock family decided to move to California. By 1920 they settled at Whittier, and he entered the building business in that city.

The First World War had given great impetus to the motor machinery business. Ambulances driven in France, the trailing of heavy siege guns behind the larger and more powerful trucks, and the general improvement in motors convinced even the most obdurate of the horsemen that the power age was here to stay. Among those who were looking ahead for developments was diminutive Lee Larrabee of Liberal, Kansas. He was a close friend of Hancock and operated a lumber yard with which Hancock had done thousands of dollars worth of business during his home construction years in that town. Hancock now approached Larrabee with a deal. For $1,500 he would give Larrabee a half-interest in his trailer idea and build a trailer that would be readily marketable. Larrabee agreed. Within a few months after his arrival in California, Charles Hancock set to work to build a salable home trailer that would attract buyers and to get it patented. In a few months he completed his first small "expandable sides" trailer house, a twelve-foot trailer that was compact, mobile, and would follow any car or truck with his new hookup without excessive sway, drag, or pull on the car.

Hancock followed his Little Trailer a few months later with a larger, family-size trailer, and to test its qualities set forth on a vacation to Canada with his wife. He was no longer afraid of mountain passes or rough prairie trails, for the auto trailers he had perfected would go anywhere a car or truck could pull them. The other trailers he had seen attempted were crude, dangerous on the road, and in no way acceptable as commercial properties for sale. But he had modeled his own trailers to meet the convenience and safety requirements of the family on tour, so he knew his models led the field.

Hancock's building enterprise had grown quickly and he was now occupied in building homes in Whittier, leaving him no time for advancing his trailer work or getting them before the public. As time continued to slip by, he decided to show his trailers at the nearby fairs, and at some of the larger fairs in southern California. At the Los Angeles County Fair the larger trailer, with its expandable sides, created great interest. Shortly after the fair was over, two representatives from the Warner Brothers Motion Picture Studios came to see him. The company was preparing to film a picture called *The Lonesome Trailer*, featuring the comedian El Brendel, costarring Edna Bennet, a popular comedienne. The Warner Brothers men told him they had seen the Little Trailer at the fair and since it would cost a high price to produce anything like it they would like to make an agreement to use it in the film.

Hancock realized that such a motion picture would throw the spotlight of national publicity on his trailers, so he readily agreed to accept their offer of $100 a day for the Little Trailer while using it in the production of the film. Hancock's son, Bud, was employed by the film company to handle the trailer and to get it to the various sets as well as to manipulate its various facilities, roll down the beds, and handle the engineering devices for expanding its sides. The Little Trailer was pulled to the studio lot by a sport model Austin roadster, creating a sensation as it passed down the streets of Los Angeles at that time, for its overall diminutive effect would even today be an attraction that would command attention, and this nearly fifty years ago!

The Lonesome Trailer was an instantaneous nationwide success, for comedian El Brendel with his Scandinavian accent was a popular star of the day. His antics in the tiny trailer with his huge dog, a wailing baby, and the lovely Edna Bennet adding to the film's interest with her charm and humor, left audiences in stitches. But it did something else, it gave everyone who saw the film a desire to own a small, compact, expandable-sides trailer just like the one they had seen in the film. Thousands of letters poured into Warner Brothers Studio, asking where such a trailer could be purchased—and this in a Depression year when the country was supposed to be down and out. It was convincing proof that there is always money to purchase an item that is needed and wanted by the public. The facts showed that the public was now ready to buy Little Trailers by the thousands.

Many manufacturers and promoters sought out the builder of the Little Trailer. Charles Edward Hancock was now past sixty years, though he appeared ten years younger and had the drive of a man of forty. He was still the honest inventor and worker, but not a sharp financier and businessman, the type needed to see plans through to a successful conclusion. And there was a serious weakness in his makeup, if such it should be called. His good friend John Baughman, who had gone on to become the nation's single largest individual landholder, had one time suggested as much to Hancock.

"Ed," Baughman said at that time (for everyone called Hancock by his second name), "you have the frank and open personality that becomes your nature. And that openness gives you the opportunity to gyp any man you do business with. But you never have done it, and never will do it. You don't ask for a signature on a note. You take every man's word for what he says. But that lays you open at times to being gypped yourself—by me, or by anyone else you do business with." In his frank and open way, John Baughman was trying to warn his friend to become more businesslike in his dealings. But Hancock, with the pioneer's manner, could never change.

"If a man's word is no good, his note is no better," he would say.

Now three sharp men, promoters, sought out Charles Hancock on a deal to manufacture and sell his Little Trailer, with the expandable sides. They promised to finance, promote, and insure the business against patent infringement, and they would also protect Lee Larrabee's investment in the trailer, they said. They laid the plans for a large manufacturing plant right there in Whittier, California, Charles Hancock's hometown, where they could build to supply the growing national market.

Hancock was impressed. The hope of ameliorating the unemployment in southern California stirred his humane senses, and he gave the three promoters full power of attorney to go ahead in any way they deemed it best to develop and manufacture the expandable-sides trailers, both large ones and the Little Trailers.

When the three promoters, "Messrs. Ketchum, Holdem, and Skinnum," Hancock later dubbed them, departed, Charles Hancock held no patent to his inventions and his years of labor were lost to him!

A thief actually steals mostly from himself. And a crooked promoter, or confidence man, however talented he may be, only promotes himself out of business. Would he but direct his abilities into honest channels, such a man would no doubt make a great fortune within the law. But in Charles Hancock's case, as in all such confidence cases, there could be but one end—failure for everyone. For the three crooks threw all of Hancock's ideas and inventions into the public domain.

"The event was so painful I find it difficult to even write about it to this day," Hancock wrote a quarter of a century later.

But Hancock's personal debacle threw open his inventions and creative efforts to all, and soon trailers such as he had perfected and ideas he had envisioned were being investigated by many other honest manufacturers, people with no connection to the three promoters and in no way responsible for Hancock's financial tragedy.

With true pioneer spirit Hancock spent no time in lamentations, but went ahead to make a good life for himself and his family in the home construction business, building scores of modern homes for his friends and customers. At the age of eighty-seven, just two years before his death, he philosophized in a letter to the writer.

True, I never made a million. Oh, I made it all right, but I never had it at one time. But I learned this, my friend, and I learned much of it through my trailers: Too much time is taken from Man's life to earn a living. Not enough time is used by him to enjoy his life.

We did take good trips, my wife and I and our family, in my trailers, and I never regretted a dime we spent in enjoying life together. The trailers helped me to free my shackles from hard carpenter work and contracting that, while well-paying, was terribly confining and trying on me.

We raised a fine family of boys and girls, and no man was ever more proud of his children or had better ones than we have. My beloved wife, Lottie Grace, has gone on ahead of us to see that we shall have a good place to stay when we join her. At age 87 I offer you this advice for what it is worth:

"Live happily and enjoy your life. Take good care of your health. If you have a good mate, love and treasure her, for that is God's finest gift to us all—a loving partner."

As Charles Hancock learned many years ago, Americans today are learning that the mobile home, whether the deluxe model or simple camper, provides a vehicle in which they can leave their worldly cares and troubles behind and set out, gypsylike, to a new world of adventures. Charles Hancock thought of his trailer idea as an extension of the covered wagon, with the comforts of home, in which he and his father's family crossed the Great Plains in 1885. This experience, at once so pleasurable and memorable to him and his family, he wanted all others to enjoy. For when you get to the Great Plains, into the mountains, or at the lakes or seashore in your trailers, you find the new life, enjoyed by the Hancocks when they first crossed the plains.

As the covered wagon of yesterday brought a new world to the pioneers of that age, so has the mobile home of today brought to our generation a multitude of its own wonders. Out on the highways and byways, in the company of family and friends, viewing the pristine loveliness that yet marks many sections of our land, you discover for yourself why she is called "America, the Beautiful."

8

Lost Pirate's Gold
at Lampasas River

J. Frank Dobie and other western writers have toyed with the
tantalizing lost treasure, but only a Texas man, A. C. Urvin, ever
touched a part of the ten-burro gold train.

J. Frank Dobie, back in the 1920s, related the curious tale of a lost gold
cache in the region of Bell, Falls, and Williamson counties, in Texas.
By the 1950s, when the writer visited several hours with Dobie at his
home in Austin, the famous folklorist and historian had learned no
more of the mysterious disappearance of the treasure. Had it not been
for my visit with Dobie, I doubt that the news story, culled from an
old issue of the *Georgetown* (Tex.) *Sun*, a paper in which I was doing
research on another subject, would ever have appealed to me or
impressed itself on my consciousness. But the visit with Dobie of the
previous day had enlarged my research, so I copied out the story
which was related therein.

The background of the full story is this: Dobie, the early secretary
of the Texas Folklore Society, had come across the story, told and
retold by pioneer people in that region, of a German, Karl Steinheimer, born near Speyer, Germany, in 1793 who ran away at age
eleven and joined up with a pirate ship. When he was in his teens,
Steinheimer commanded his own pirate craft with a partner, Aury.
The two young men broke over a question of piratical "policy," and
Steinheimer gave up piracy and journeyed into the Sierra Madre
mountains of Mexico and found gold in great quantities, becoming a
rich man.

In 1838, how is not explained, he learned that a boyhood sweetheart he had known on the Mexican Gulf in his youthful pirate days
was in St. Louis and still, like himself, unmarried. He sent word to

her that he was going to St. Louis, closed up his affairs, loaded a fortune of silver and gold, with many gold coins, on ten Mexican burros. With two hired guards in whom he had faith, he started in the general direction of Missouri.

At Matamoras he learned that notwithstanding the defeat of Mexican General Santa Anna, at San Jacinto, nearly three years before, Mexico still hoped to repossess Texas by arms. Preliminary to the proposed conquest, Manuel Flores and a handful of men were preparing to start from Matamoras to Nacogdoches, in 1839, to foment an Indian uprising against the colonists and settlers. Steinheimer joined with this band. At the Colorado River they were dismayed to learn that General Burleson was advancing upon them for a battle the next morning. Upon agreement with Flores, Steinheimer that night left the command with his two men and their ten mule loads, beginning a detour to the north several miles. Flores, history reveals, proceeded to a point near Austin where, in battle with a detachment under Lieutenant James O. Rice, he was killed on 14 May, and his small band broken up or killed.

Steinheimer picked his way carefully across the prairies, camping nights in the bosques and thickets of post oak trees. One day they came to a place where three streams intersected. Here, according to Dobie's story, the former pirate decided to bury all of his fortune except enough to afford him his immediate needs and to reward his two faithful men and keep them in his employ. The only sign he left to mark the buried treasure was a heavy boat spike, driven into a large oak tree a few yards from the site. Then Steinheimer and his men set out in a southerly direction and, within fourteen miles, came to a "bunch of knobs on the prairie." Here, they were attacked by Indians and the German's two faithful guards were killed in the ambush. Badly wounded, Steinheimer concealed himself near the center hill, burying his remaining gold with the exception of six Spanish coins which he would need for food. After a few days, feeling strength again, he continued his journey southeastward and fell in with a party of travelers heading east.

Though Steinheimer had survived, his wounds told him he would die eventually, so he drew up a crude map of the region where he had buried his wealth and wrote his sweetheart an account of his travail and misfortune. He requested that she keep the matter secret for three months, and if at the close of that time he had not appeared in St. Louis, she was to assume he was dead and that the fortune would be hers. This was the last known of Steinheimer, for he never appeared in St. Louis although the message and map reached the girl after a period of time.

Recruiting family members who could make the trip, the girl had a party of her menfolk search the knobs area, that distinctly marked region between present Elgin and Lexington, Texas, where three good-sized eminences appear as green "knobs" on the horizon, for the lesser treasure, hoping that the well-defined geography, and terrain, as described by Steinheimer's map would offer them a better opportunity for discovery than the vague reference to the "three streams," which, if his directions were accurate, could only be the junctions of the Nolan, the Lampasas, and the Leon rivers. Nothing was located after a search over the knobs area. The search party moved on to the confluences of the three rivers. After a long, difficult, and tiring hunt, the search was abandoned, and the party returned to St. Louis. What happened to the map, and the letter, has never been revealed. It was later written, "No evidence exists that any part of Steinheimer's wealth was ever found, despite the great amount of time and money spent in its quest." To this, Mr. J. Frank Dobie agreed, the day I visited with him in the 1950s at Austin.

However, there is a sequel to the above as revealed in the old newspaper story mentioned earlier in the *Georgetown* (Tex.) *Sun*, 13 August, 1885. Just half-way between Waco and Austin, Texas, is the town of Belton. Neaby flow the rivers mentioned on the treasure map of the German. The Leon and Lampasas rivers flow through the Turnbo neighborhood, as it was called in the 1860s, near "Younsport," which, since it no longer appears on maps must be a ghost town, or at best, a small country crossroads village today. In that vicinity, in the late 1870s there were traditions of buried gold and the many stories drew attention to this locality. But the people who lived in the vicinity gave little credence to the folktales, for they had heard them since childhood.

One day three Mexican *marineros* came to the region. They began by searching the area along the river near the McBride settlement, frequently digging with pick and shovel, then moving upstream and downstream, yet always within an area of fifty *varas* of the spot where they initially commenced their search. Their activities drew much attention from the residents of the community, for their seamen's uniforms set them apart like a red scarf on a blanket of snow. The *marineros* were closemouthed men, talked as little as possible when questioned, but appeared pleased to answer the questions put to them. They revealed one thing: they were searching for buried gold in stone jars, and three chests of *cargemento de navio*.

The residents watched the searchers for ten days as the *marineros* paced off distances, checked their compass, and hacked deep holes into the ground on the stream banks. One day the *marineros* packed up and left as secretly and silently as they had come. But they had found no gold, for the residents, watching day and night from concealment in the brush and trees never saw them load anything that resembled treasure.

A decade passed, then another. The residents who had seen the *marineros* make their search were now snow-thatched, their children in their middle age. One of the younger men of the vicinity was a man named A. C. Urvin. His father resided in Burnet County. The son, a good enough chap, lived around the region, working for first one farmer, then another, or at odd jobs in the small towns.

One day young Urvin decided to visit his father at Bertram. In traveling from the Turnbo's, where he was employed at the time, he cut across the McBride settlement, crossing the Lampasas River. After making the crossing, afoot, he sat down upon what he thought to be a mud-covered stump to wring out his socks. As he sat there, the stump appeared to be strange to him, round on the top, as though man-made. He examined the top of it, and found it to be the cover of an *old stone jar*! Prying loose the lid, and breaking it away from the jar, he peered within. The large churn-sized jar was filled to the brim with gold coins of many sizes and descriptions, all stained with age, but intact. Taking up a fistful, he saw that several dated back to 1671 and had Spanish legends upon them.

Now Urvin became sly, aware that he had uncovered great wealth.

Taking out a handful, he carefully replaced the broken top, covered the "stump" with more mud and with brush. Then he continued on to his father's place.

That evening, a neighbor named John Harte from Florence, was visiting at the elder Urvin's home. During the course of the evening he discovered Urvin counting and inspecting his gold coins. Urvin, surprised, confessed he had won the gold playing poker. But Harte did not believe him, and he later told a Mr. Stanley of his disbelief. Soon, many folks in the Burnet County area had learned of the gold coins Urvin possessed, and the talk in the community grew.

A. C. Urvin had a brother who was at his father's home that evening. The two brothers returned to the scene of the buried treasure the following morning leading a saddle horse with two *morrals*, or nosebags, thrown over the saddle. At the location, they filled each nosebag half full of gold coins, then again covered the jar with mud and brush. When they returned to Bertram, they told a Mr. Eugene Gahn and a man named McDonald of their discovery. These two men spread the story.

At Belton, the story did not travel far until it reached the ears of Moses Whitsitt. He went immediately to the *Belton Journal*, telling the editor that young Urvin was covering up a theft of gold coins he had taken from a merchant named Atkinson of Florence, a nearby town, who had lost a collection of rare gold coins. Whitsitt made the further charge that A. C. Urvin had an alias of Maxwell, which he used at times.

Now it has never been learned whether the man Whitsitt and the merchant Atkinson connived to bring themselves into possession of Urvin's treasure. But it did appear that way. For A. C. Urvin made a strong defense of himself in a letter that was published in the *Georgetown* (Tex.) *Sun*, Thursday, 13 August, 1885, written from Holland, Texas, where Urvin was at that time. Urvin wrote:

> Dear Sirs:
>
> I found $11,300.00 in Old Spanish coin and have it now in U.S. money. As to my name, it is A. C. Urvin. I have both father and mother, and two brothers to prove my connections. I am now living in the neighborhood of Hol-

land, with G. T. Smith. I am no thief or robber. I will be
in Belton this week and see you. I can prove as good a
character, from my childhood down to this time as any
man in Texas.
Yours truly,
A. C. Urvin

Urvin's letter apparently broke the back of any conspiracy to mulct
him of his discovery, for nothing was later charged to him. But it
failed to answer the question as to what happened to the rest of the
pirate's treasure buried on the Lampasas River. Did Urvin return to
discover the remaining chests of treasure in silver and gold, of which
he was totally unaware when he made his initial discovery? Or do the
rotting sea chests and pottery jars still hide their secret, near the great
oak with the boat spike that now, itself, lies buried by the years in the
heart of the oak tree? Or did the stories of the pirate gold start up *after*
Urvin's discovery of the treasure of gold coins, in 1885? As the
Spanish residents of the region said, when I asked about the treasure,
and Urvin, "¿Quien sabe" ("Who knows?")

9

The Johnson–Eldridge Feud in No Man's Land

A feud of ninety years ago finally explained.

In 1887 and 1888 the Grangers poured into the Public Land Strip, the area now known as the Oklahoma Panhandle. It was then unclaimed by any state or territory and was a land without law of any kind. The complete lawlessness, with many murders and lynchings, had brought about the organization of vigilante groups, some of them lawless and vicious enough to be considered on a par with the worst criminals in that land.

Among the recent arrivals to the land at this time were two families, the Johnsons and the Eldridges. The Eldridges arrived first, and settled on two quarter-sections of land on the north bank of the Beaver River, near the sod town of Grand Valley, where one vigilante group of little worth made its headquarters. This village was being promoted by the Scranage faction of Beaver City, a larger town situated down the river a few miles.

The Johnsons, coming a few months later, were unable to find unoccupied land bordering the river so they took up a dry land claim to the north, but adjoining the Eldridge land.

The land, of course, was claimed only by squatter's rights, for it was impossible to homestead land about which the title was uncertain.

Since the Johnsons had no well or watering place they were obliged to get consent from the Eldridge family to cross their land and haul water from the river and to water their livestock there. But the senior member of the Eldridge family, William H. Eldridge, was an obliging man, and a neighborly pattern was at first established between the families.

Within a few weeks, however, several matters arose to cause the two families to bicker and quarrel. The Johnsons let their horses graze at will, for it was all free range, and the animals naturally drifted down on to the river bottom and the better grass of the Eldridge pasture, for there were no fences to stop them.

The Eldridges, gathering surface coal (the cow chips) for winter fuel, gathered over the Johnson land, where their own cattle grazed. For, they reasoned, since the Johnsons owned no cattle but a milk cow, the Eldridge cattle had created the winter fuel on the prairie.

Such trivial matters assumed great importance to poverty-stricken settlers who had little or nothing of the world's goods and were attempting to scratch a living from this sun-baked and arid land. As the minor squabbles continued and multiplied, they set the stage for the tragedies that were to follow. For the toughness and meanness exhibited by one family or the other elicited only a reciprocal meanness and toughness from its neighbor.

One evening a traveling evangelist conducted a prayer meeting, speaking in a neighbor's soddy in that area. Both the Johnsons and the Eldridges attended, for both were devoutly Christian families. During the services two of the Johnson boys, Charley, age twenty, and Frankie, age nineteen, began heckling the preacher, who sermonized a bit off the Fundamentalist position which they knew. The elder member of the Eldridge family permitted his two stalwart sons to assume the roles of peacekeepers of the tabernacle, and the Eldridge boys, with some difficulty, forcibly ejected the Johnson boys from the soddy.

This assault upon his sons did not sit well with the elder Johnson and he spoke some harsh words to the Eldridge boys' father about it, which brought about retribution in the form of W. H. Eldridge's denial of his land and water to the Johnsons, causing them to have to drive their stock west a mile to water near a ford on the stream.

Sometime later Ben, the younger Eldridge son, who was then fourteen, was watering their cattle at the river when the two Johnson boys rode up within a few rods, taking their horses to water at the stream. The Johnson boys were armed with a 50-caliber Sharps rifle and began taking potshots in the direction of the lad. They probably tried, or intended, only to scare him, for they shot six or eight times, no bullet coming closer than ten or fifteen feet to him as he lay under a clay bank for protection. But two of those missiles struck two of the Eldridge cows standing in the background, wounding them so severely they had to be destroyed.

When Ben Eldridge returned home and told his father about the shooting, old Will Eldridge was furious. Si and Marion joined him, and when they suggested an armed attack on the Johnson home, the father's anger overcame his reason.

"I'll not only let you, I'll go with you and we'll teach those puppies a good lesson in manners," he told his sons, taking his old 50-caliber buffalo rifle from its pegs on the sod wall.

The Eldridge boys armed themselves with their six-shooters and the trio set out for the Johnson soddies—there were two of them, and the sod walls of their corral—on the prairie.

The Eldridges left their horses to graze on the prairie and continued the last quarter mile afoot, walking directly to the sod wall being laid up for a windbreak by the Johnson boys who were at that time carrying sod from a wagon. At the approach of the Eldridges, the two Johnson boys fled to the house, soon followed by their father and other members of their family who were in the yeard. The Eldridges took up a position behind the nearest sod wall and there began firing at the sod house.

At first the Johnsons returned their fire from the windows of the house. But soon they realized that some of their womenfolk would be hurt if they remained inside and drew the Eldridge fire into their home, so they took up new positions, one by one, behind a sod corral wall near the house.

During the exchanges of bullets at this time, Si Eldridge was struck in the neck with a 50-caliber bullet from the Sharps rifle being used by Charley Johnson. The bullet entered Eldridge's neck and came out alongside his chin.

Marion and his father now realized the tragic turn the fight had taken and sought to withdraw from the scene of the battle. They finally succeeded in getting the seriously wounded Si away from the

Johnson place, amid a hail of bullets, and back to their own home. But the terrible wound inflicted by the big rifle was too great, and that night Si Eldridge died in agony. Two days later he was buried, the entire community for miles around attending the services, all but the Johnsons.

The news of this gun battle swept the little community like a prairie fire, for, as in most areas of the West, every family had its friends and the Johnsons and Eldridges were well known to many, most neighbors being on good terms with both of the families. This probably kept the two-family feud from spreading among the neighbors.

There was, at this time, a second factor that played a most important part in keeping the feud from reaching out into other parts of the community. The newly created Vigilance Committee at Grand Valley served the interests of the Beaver City land sharks in that area and was under the leadership of a local man named Davis, a character so unpopular that the settlers nicknamed him "Puke" Davis.

He was a tall, gaunt fellow with a red beard and the fierce-glinting eyes of the born zealot. Many settlers feared him and his night riders. When the news of the shooting reached his ears, he called up his court and drew up an order instructing the Johnsons and the Eldridges to leave the Public Land Strip or pay the Committee a fine of twenty-five dollars each "for disturbing the peace."

The fine was, of course, pure graft and nonsense, for the Vigilantes had no more authority in law than did the Eldridges or Johnsons to force others off their claims or to pay tribute. But their lynch practices had established them as the only "law" at that time.

The Johnsons had no money with which to pay, but stayed on a month or more, untroubled by the vigilantes. But the committee maintained steady pressure on the Eldridges, eventually forcing them to agree to leave. The Johnsons, then, packed up and left. As the Johnson wagons moved eastward, near Beaver City, in the deepening dusk, Charley was perched on the seat of the lead wagon, driving a four-horse team. Peering ahead up the trail road, he spotted a horse tied in some cottonwood trees near the bank of the river, not far from the road. Charley drew up his team, called back to his father on the second wagon and asked him to hold his horses while he went up the road to investigate. Slipping his Winchester from the scabbard which hung on the front bow of the wagon, Charley stepped down from the seat and started walking ahead up the trail.

After a few minutes the waiting family members heard the report of a rifle, then two more shots sounded in the still air. Johnson and son Frankie scouted up the road, well-armed, and moving cautiously to avoid being bushwhacked in the dark. At a curve in the road they found Charley's body between the wagon ruts, lying on his back. He had been shot once in the back, twice in the breast.

The Johnson family stopped at Beaver City for a few days while they buried their son, and today Charley's body rests on the round, windswept hill southwest of Beaver, Oklahoma, one of the first graves in that cemetery. While at Beaver City the Johnsons tried hard to establish who had shot Charley, and for what reason. Naturally, they suspected the Eldridges, but no evidence could be found and the Eldridge family gave valid proof that they had all been at home on that night. The Johnsons continued on and eventually found good farms for themselves in the Cherokee Strip.

Back in No Man's Land, the citizens who were friendly to the Eldridges felt strongly that the family had been driven away from their home for no good reason. The father, William Eldridge, though remaining in the strip himself, had taken his family to a safe place across the Texas line, out of the way of the vigilantes. The neighbors were now circulating a petition, asking the Vigilante Committee to reconsider its position and permit the Eldridges to return to their home.

Although the committee, headed by "Puke" Davis, seemed to represent the only "power" in the community, it was at a crucial time when their power was being challenged by the bolder cowmen, especially the Hardesty cowboys, and others in the area. One wiry settler, Oliver M. Nelson, had at that time sent his personal challenge to the committee, after its members had stolen everything in his sod dugout while he was away from home a few days. Ollie simply armed himself with a neighbor's Long Tom buffalo rifle, his own six-shooter, and other assorted weapons and set forth to bring about justice "or put a dozen thieves sleeping under the sod." Ollie was backed by a couple of tough brothers.

When the petition was presented to Nelson, he wryly suggested that the Eldridges arm themselves again, join with him, and with the backing of the Hardesty cowboys, led by Tom Hungate, they would run the vigilantes out of the Public Land Strip. But Will Eldridge had lost one son, and the contentiousness of the various factions would bring more deaths, he knew. So instead he joined with the more peaceful elements of the community and continued to circulate their petition, which read:

TO WHOM IT MAY CONCERN

We, the undersigned citizens of Shade County, Public Land Strip, believing that W. H. Eldridge and sons have been unfairly dealt with by having to remove from The Strip, while the Johnson family, if not the aggressors, are equally guilty, (and) have been allowed by a higher power to remain against the expressed wishes of a majority of the citizens.

Now in view of the above facts we do advise and ask W. H. Eldridge and sons to return to Shade County at any time they may deem it to their interests to do so:

Signed: H. A. Frank; Wm. H. Talcott; Joseph Young; Will Ewing; John Rose; E. B. Mitchell; J. M. Clover; J. W. Mitchell; A. B. Mitchell, A. E. Jackson; J. H. [name unreadable]; J. W. Frank, Wm. Bailey, R. Handkins; G. W. Speese; W. K. Byram; J. S. Hungate; T. H. Colver; John Davis; M. Yowell; A. J. Hower; W. A. Sullivan; J. H. Clover; Franklin Dolliarie; O. W. Wilson; B. O. Shallenbarger; A. J. Walkup; Boss Neff, Ira Neff; John Burns; E. H. Stalnaker; J. H. Dadiman.
Hardesty, I. T., March 27, 1889
(Sgd.) Andrew Howenstein, Court Judge

By the time the petition was closed and ready for presentation to "Puke" Davis's committee they had all fled or had indicated their willingness to cease night riding and plundering. W. H. Eldridge was invited to return to his home with his family. The newly established court judge for "Shade County," (present Texas County, Oklahoma) now having no one to whom he could present the petition, handed it to W. H. Eldridge with his compliments as a testimonial of the friends who stood by him in No Man's Land. When the father died, he passed the document along to his son, Marion W. Eldridge, Sr. Young Marion was then eighteen years old, and he kept the paper for many years and passed it along to his son, the late Marion W. Eldridge, Jr., of Gridley, California, who provided much of the information concerning the feud.

Following the return of the Eldridge family to the strip, son Marion went to work for the Hardesty ranch. The Hardesty cowboys had backed the Eldridges in their dispute with the vigilantes, though remaining neutral in the feud beteen the two settler families. Marion, Sr., became foreman of the Hardesty ranch in due time and, when Col. Jack Hardesty withdrew from the cattle range in the nineties, he acquired the quarter-section of land where the old ranch headquarters buildings had stood. There he later constructed a good stone house. This is now Twp. 1, R-19, Sec. 23, NW 1/4, in what is today, Texas County, the panhandle of Oklahoma.

Marion W. Eldridge, Sr., lived there with his family until drought and hard times forced them off the land in 1909, but the old man retained possession of his acreage.

Now fine wheat and maize fields grace the prairie where the Johnsons and the Eldridges shot it out with Sharps buffalo rifles and six-shooters. Only in the memories of their descendants are these dramatic incidents of our pioneer history recalled.

The fierce and bitter struggle for a landhold waged by these two pioneer families ended in a double tragedy that is now a part of the history of old No Man's Land.

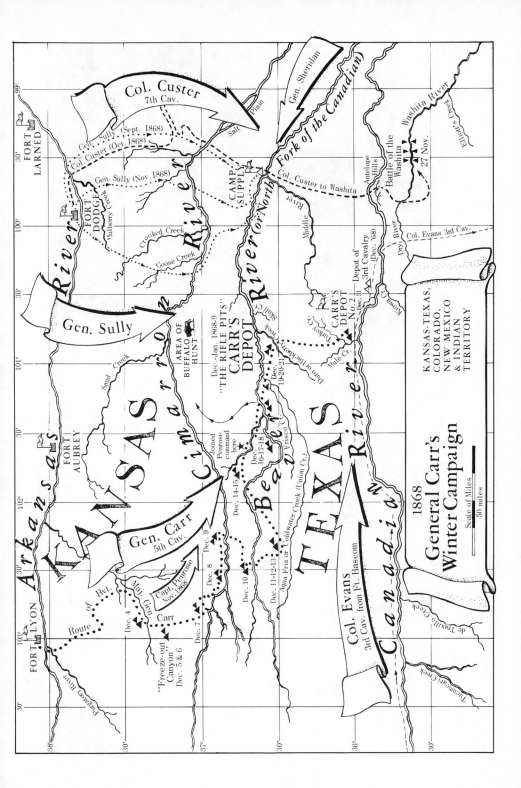

A seven-foot pole sinks into a Devil's cattle trap pit all the way! Jon Brammier, shown holding the pole, was once rescued from a pit he'd stepped into. (*Photo courtesy* The Scottsbluff (*Neb.*) Star-Herald.)

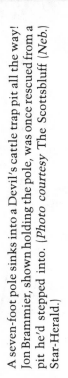

This trailer with expandable sides (below), invented by Charles E. Hancock, was the forerunner of the gigantic fifth wheelers of today. It was featured in a motion picture, "The Little Trailer," in 1935. El Brendel, a popular comedian of the time, appeared in the film. (*Photo courtesy* Warner Brothers Studios.)

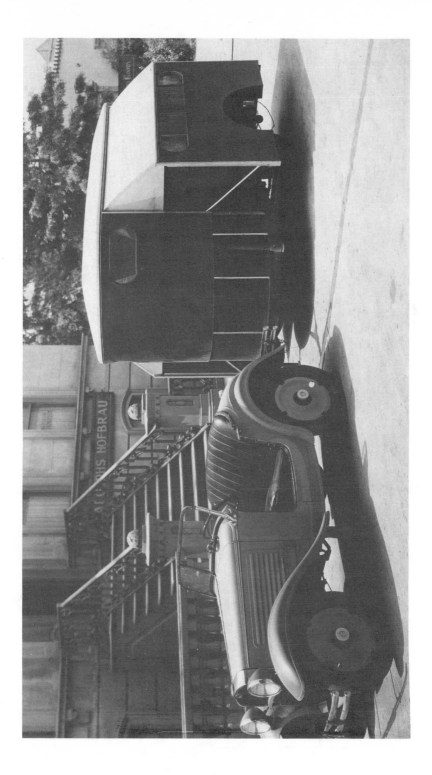

Official maps of the West and Southwest during the time of Jedediah Smith were vague and uncertain. The section shown here, extracted and redrawn by the author from a map published with Congressional H.R. 474, dated May 20, 1834, shows the Cimarron (not named on the original) making its confluence with the Arkansas in the vicinity of what is now Cimarron, Kansas.

The map below shows the routes of the two crossings of the "Cimarron Desert" by Jedediah Smith in 1818 and 1831. The great southeastern drop made by the Cimarron River was uncharted in Smith's time (see map at left). Its course was confused by the explorers with the twists and turns of Crooked Creek.

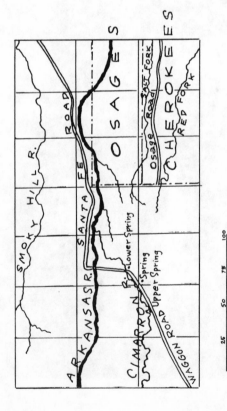

Scale = 100 Miles

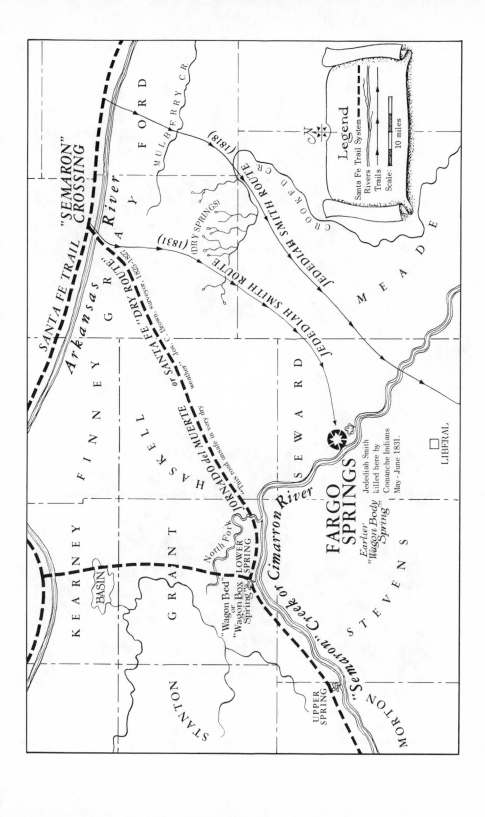

SANTA FE TRAIL

"SEMARON" CROSSING

Arkansas River

Arkansas River

GRAY FORD

MULBERRY CR.

(1818)

(DRY SPRINGS)

(1831)

CROOKED CR.

JEDEDIAH SMITH ROUTE

JEDEDIAH SMITH ROUTE

FINNEY

KEARNEY

HASKELL

"DRY ROUTE" 1825-1827

or SANTA FE "JORNADO del MUERTE"

weather; Jos. C. Brown, surveyor.

"this road unsafe in very dry

BASIN

North Fork

"Wagon Bed" or "Wagon Box" Spring

LOWER SPRING

GRANT

STANTON

"Semaron" Creek or Cimarron River

UPPER SPRING

SEWARD

MEADE

LIBERAL

FARGO SPRINGS

Earlier "Wagon Body Spring"

Jedediah Smith killed here by Comanche Indians May - June 1831.

STEVENS

MORTON

Legend

Santa Fe Trail System

Rivers

Trails

Scale: 10 miles

N

Captain James H. Cook—former trail driver, Army Scout, Indian fighter, and hunter—at the Agate Springs Fossil Quarry, about 1918. (*Photo courtesy Mrs. Harold Cook.*)

Leroy F. Dick, who trailed the two Bender women to Michigan and returned them to Kansas for trial. (*Courtesy Kansas State Historical Society, Topeka, Kansas.*)

Southwest view of the Bender place in Kansas, showing spectators in the area where the bodies of the victims were discovered in unmarked graves. The small building in the background is the Bender house. (*Photo by G. R. Gamble. Courtesy Kansas State Historical Society.*)

10

Aunt Babe

(1872–1974)

A fascinating frontier character who defeated blizzards and sickness and lived to be 102 years of age. The following was written about her in 1967.

Miss Ruth Chrisman, "Aunt Babe" as she is affectionately known in our family, is a wrinkled and careworn little woman of ninety-five years. She is now stooped from her labors of the past, and her hands are twisted by painful arthritis. She carries a cane on occasions when she has to walk down her porch steps.

Aunt Babe lives alone, for she never married. She does her own cooking, tends to her own housework, does her own grooming, and even mows her lawn with an old-fashioned hand power mower. But one thing stands out in her above all other characteristics—she is young in spirit. Although she is nearly blind, her nieces and her nephews marvel at her toughness, that strength common among pioneers, and most of us agree that she has a good chance to pass 100 years.

Aunt Babe's toughness is understandable when you reflect upon how the pioneers who came west survived the environment in which they lived while they developed the fine farms and ranches we see in the West today. Aunt Babe's folks were Virginians, and the family roots go far back into the history of the Old South prior to Revolutionary times.

On a recent visit I made to her home in Broken Bow, Nebraska, she dredged up incidents from her memory she had heard told about Civil War times by family members. Suddenly she broke out into a song of that period:

And here's to brave Virginia, the old Dominion state—
With the young Confederacy at length has linked her
fate—Impelled by her example, now other states prepar'—
To hoist on high the Bonnie Blue Flag that bears a single
star.

In 1879, when she was seven years old, and big enough to help drive
the team on her father's covered wagon, Aunt Babe migrated with her
family from their old home near Waverly, Missouri, where she was
born, to Nebraska. But let's let her tell it, as she told it to me a few
weeks ago:

> We seven children were all born in Lafayette County,
> Missouri, on the old plantation where grandfather Joseph
> Chrisman settled in 1837, after moving from Edom, in
> Rockingham County, Virginia. He and grandmother rode
> all that distance in his fine old Rockaway carriage.
>
> Now the time that I recall as a small child in Missouri
> was the period of the post-Civil War years. Guerrillas had
> overrun the area, and some of grandfather's slaves had run
> away and joined the Union Army. Alex Clark and William
> Bowlin were two of them. But several of the black men
> stayed on with us, and under the guidance of old Uncle
> Adam Stepp they grew enough food to care for all of our
> families, negroe and white.
>
> Our first school there was Mount Hope, a log cabin in
> the woods. On the way home from school the children
> would gather wild flowers and berries. My brothers and
> sisters learned to tap dance and do the soft-shoe on that
> little wooden bridge that spanned a stream. They were
> taught the steps by the little negro boys of the neighbor-
> hood, then they taught them to me. I have always loved
> to dance since then, and later attended many barn dances
> and other social affairs on the plains where dancing was a
> favorite recreation. It was good for all of us, young and
> old.
>
> Our old Missouri home was a large, two-story brick
> mansion with a sugar trim all around. The bricks were
> made right there on the place. Along the lane leading up

to the house was a long row of cherry trees, and grand-father had planted a fine twenty-acre apple orchard.

My father, Joseph Marcus Chrisman, fed and shipped cattle. I recall the lovely gifts he brought back from St. Louis. Once he brought sidesaddles for the older girls, for ladies then rode only sideways, with long riding skirts to cover the feet and ankles. Grandmother Jane could always tell when father did well at the market, for he brought back many gifts at those times for the family.

At this time, about 1875 to 1878, father was not doing well in his cattle business. He had heard of the western lands that were open for homesteads. He made a tour of inspection, then returned and we packed up six covered wagons, loaded all our household goods, took all our peo-ple, colored and white, and moved to eastern Nebraska. We settled temporarily at Stella, near Brownsville, in Nemaha County.

After a year or two father again decided to move farther west, since he had not exercised his homestead option yet. Again we packed up the wagons and gathered the live-stock and set forth to Custer County, in central Nebraska. Father had gone to Texas and purchased several hundred head of purebred Durham cattle. These he shipped to Kearney, Nebraska, and my three brothers, Ab, Mack, and Genie, trailed them to Custer County. But my! What a difficult time they had pulling bogged cattle out of those streams!

Father wanted mother to remain at Kearney and see that we girls got through that school term, but mother ruled that where father and the three boys went, there we would all go. "The family must stay together," I often heard her say. So we all left Kearney together.

When we crossed the low wooden bridge that spanned the Platte River, some ducks that had been resting under the structure flew up, their wings making a terrific flapping noise that scared the teams. Those mules that we were driving stood straight up and pawed the air ahead of us. When I lost control of them father quickly grabbed the

lines from me and straightened out the team. But I was
scared speechless, although unhurt.

We arrived at Broken Bow in May of 1882. It was just a
sod town with a few frame buildings being erected into
both homes and commercial places. One old soddy with
the top plastered over with cement to keep it from leaking
was called The Marble Top Hotel!

There was a post office, operated by a Mr. Wilson
Hewitt. He had found a broken Indian bow in 1880 and
had petitioned for the post office to be named after that
incident.

Our ranch was established on father's homestead near
the head of Lillian Creek, twenty miles north of the town,
and he ran his cattle on what was still free range.

That first winter was a terribly cold one, our cattle were
unseasoned, and we did not have sufficient winter feed for
them, or good shelter. We lost nearly a third of them in
the storms. That following year father and the boys built
sod shelters, corrals and a good, warm sod house for the
family. It was later said that, "Those Chrismans laid up
enough sod in '83 to fence Custer County."

The boys also hauled cedar timber from the canyons
along the Dismal River for other buildings and for fences.
That third winter, 1885–86, was the worst ever seen on
the Great Plains. It took a terrible toll of our cattle, along
with all other ranchers' and settlers' stock. For despite the
sod shelters and enough feed, the cattle smothered with
ice balls on their muzzles and died in the canyon drifts.

It was a terrible loss to our family, and we were all depressed over it. Mother, who never had wanted to move
west, was almost sick with grief, although she tried to
conceal her feelings from us. We children were young and
able to accept the changes better than our elders.

One by one, as they came of age, my sisters and
brothers took up homesteads; first Lizzie, then Ab, then
Lutie, Mack, Genie, and, finally, Hattie, my next oldest
sister. But I was too young to qualify, and by the time I

was of age the land was all taken, at least the better parts. So I had to look around for work.

On January 12, 1888, I was teaching school in a small soddy four miles from father's home place, where I was staying. I was just a girl near seventeen, and had no education myself except what I had been able to obtain in the little country schools our people had established. But I wanted to make some money to help out at home, and they needed some kind of a teacher there.

That day was like Indian summer, and when I left home in the morning my brothers Ab and Genie had already gone to cut plum bush for fuel from the canyons about two miles from father's place.

Lizzie, my eldest sister, had ridden her mare, called Jessie, to the Haumont place for a visit, for the day was so beautiful no one expected a change in the weather. None of them even took coats. I always carried my coat tied behind the saddle, and I rode back and forth from my school on Daisy, another fine little mustang mare.

In the afternoon I was attending my duties in the schoolhouse. I felt a cold draft come in through the doorway, so I stepped to the door to close it. I noticed that Daisy, who was tied at the hitchrack, was acting very strangely. I usually slipped the bit from her mouth and piled some prairie hay on the ground for her to eat. Now I saw that she was going to rub the bridle off if I did not fix it, so I stepped outside to adjust her bridle. She was very nervous, and I glanced around and noticed a gray, misty cloud on the northwest horizon. The wind was very, very cold. Could there be a blizzard coming?

I returned to the soddy and took up my duties, but I was drawn to the window on the west. Now I could see snowflakes swirling ahead of the wind, which had increased. Father had warned us all, time after time, about blizzards, and counseled us to never take any chances in them.

There was not enough fuel in the building to last

through the night, and only a very meager supply outside in the woodbox, so I knew I must get the children home at once.

I told them there was a storm coming and we would dismiss school for the day. But I cautioned them to remain with me, for we would go to my home where their parents could find them after the storm. When each had his hat and coat on, I led them to the hitchrack and untied Daisy. The little mare was almost frantic now, but calmed down as soon as I released her. I tied the right rein to the saddle horn, grasped the left rein and the left stirrup in my right hand and then took hold of the largest girl's hand, telling the children to all join hands. The wind was now roaring around the building, and the snow was beginning to drive so hard against my face that I wondered if we could face it back to father's place. "Take us home, Daisy," I said to the mare, and tried to guide her northward. She faced into the bitter wind only a few minutes, then turned and reversed her direction. I could not guide her, and she returned to the schoolhouse.

I feared that she was afraid of the storm and wanted only to be near the school building, but she passed it by and headed directly south with the storm. There was nothing to do but let her go her way, for father had often told us to trust the instinct and intelligence of our saddle horses if we were lost. So we set forth into the white darkness of that storm, about the worst blizzard Nebraska ever knew.

I let Daisy walk as fast as the smallest child could travel. That next hour or two seemed endless, and I stopped three or four times to help the children who were crying from the cold. Soon I had put the three smallest ones on Daisy's back and we traveled faster, though I was afraid they might freeze while not exercising themselves in such bitter cold.

As a third hour passed and the children were becoming exhausted from walking in the drifting snow that was now a foot deep on the level places, I too, began to doubt whether any of us would live through the ordeal. Our faces were becoming frosted gray white and our hands were numb with the cold. I had stopped to try to place another child on Daisy's back when I glimpsed a dark object through the swirling snow. It was a sod house!

Quickly I led Daisy and my chain of children around to the single door, pounded on it with all my strength and cried out to those inside to help us. A woman let us inside, but it was several minutes before I could see well enough to recognize her. She was Mrs. Hickman, who lived nearly nine miles south from father's place. I knew then that our faithful Daisy had guided us straight to this place of safety, knowing that she could not get us home in the teeth of the blizzard.

When I was able I went outside, led Daisy into an adjoining shed, found some prairie hay for her to eat and melted some snow for drinking water for her.

Mrs. Hickman was busy thawing out the children, rubbing them, and slapping their hands to start the circulation. The little ones cried pitifully, but I was grateful that we were out of the storm. There was little fuel in the Hickman home and it soon became necessary to burn the chairs to keep from freezing, for the temperature dropped far below zero, and they said later that it was twenty-five degrees below zero that night. We closed off the bedroom and put all the children together, with Mrs. Hickman's three little ones, on the floor near the stove on the mattress, using all the bedclothes in the house. That night we all suffered terribly from the cold, and I had frozen my thumbs.

The following morning we divided a gooseberry pie for breakfast, for there was little food in the house, except some oatmeal. Mr. Hickman had gone to town after supplies and had not returned through the storm.

The storm never abated for three days. When we finally emerged, the soddy was covered over with a huge drift.

The contrast between the blackness of the soddy and the brilliant white world outside was blinding. But it was no doubt the great drift that saved us, for it prevented the wind from reaching us after that first terrible night. We had been able to melt snow to drink, but even the dry oatmeal had run out the second day, and we were all very hungry.

When the storm was over, the settlers and ranchers combed the country looking for their children and of course soon found us. For my pupils it was a most happy reunion. We had been very lucky, as that blizzard became known as "The Schoolchildren's Storm," because so very many children were lost in it and perished.

When all of my wards had been found by their parents, I saddled Daisy and returned home across that vast, deep white carpet of ice and snow that covered everything to a depth of two feet in most places.

As my little mare slipped and skidded down the steep hill that rose near father's soddy, Cousin Kate Richardson, who had been caught there in the blizzard while visiting, came running out to meet me. "Lawsy day, child," she cried out, taking me in her arms and helping me from the saddle, "we all thought we had lost you."

All of my people were safe, though some had felt the bite of that blizzard themselves when caught out in it. It was one of the most wonderful experiences of my life to return safely to the arms of my family.

As I grew older I was asked continually to help out with the sick of the area, especially the young country women during childbirth. Later, when I moved to Broken Bow, I became a nurse for Dr. C. L. Mullins. He was an early day practitioner who went to the homes of the sick, as was the custom of the times, and attended any one who called for him. No person who has worked beside those country doctors can have anything but the deepest respect and admiration for them.

We would set out in a light buggy behind a team. Sometimes the trips would last three or four days and we would change off one of us driving while the other got in some sleep, sitting up in the buggy seat. On some occasions, when the doctor assigned me to a case, I would stay on it several weeks while he returned home.

I have helped Dr. Mullins and other doctors deliver hundreds of babies. I have, in some cases, started to make the delivery myself, but fortunately the doctor always arrived in the nick of time.

I have been in homes where smallpox, diptheria, measles, chicken pox, and other contagious diseases prevailed but the Lord was always with me and I never contracted a fatal one.

I had one extraordinary case where a child was born in the home without the attention of a doctor. When I was called to attend the sick baby I found it had been born without a rectum. By the quickest of action, and through the dexterity of the doctor whom I immediately got to the home, an operation was performed that saved its life.

The frontier was an ample producer of injuries from accidents. Horses threw the men, and the cattle ran over them; children had bad falls from haylofts and into old wells; people were gored by bulls; and burns from using kerosene to start fires were only a part of it.

Two children drank kerosene from cans, thinking it was water. A runaway team caused a man to be dragged and terribly bruised, with many broken bones. There were an assortment of broken bones, from noses caused by fighting and bronc riding to toes twisted and broken in machinery. I learned to bandage and treat them all.

In 1918, during the terrible epidemic of Spanish influenza, I learned of a family of six near Ansley who were all ill in bed with the exception of a five-year-old boy. The neighbors had all become sick and could not help them and the doctors were already working twenty hours a day.

I hired a boy to take me there in his buggy. When I entered the home I found the mother and father and three children deathly sick, and I held little hope for the unconscious and delirious mother. I could do only what Dr. Mullins had told me, in a general way, to do. But I set to work, the small boy following me like a faithful dog, so I put him to work helping me.

He carried chambers, brought water from the outdoor well, ran little errands, and performed duties just like a male nurse would have done. One day I missed him. I searched everywhere, and finally found him curled up behind the base burner stove in the front room. I felt his hot, dry brow, and knew the worst had happened. He, too, had the dreadful flu. I had lost my only helper.

I put the child in bed beside his mother and stayed on alone. Gradually the father became better, arose from his bed and though weak and dizzy started to help me. Then the mother rallied. Within a few more days all the children, including my tiny helper, were on the road to recovery.

When I left, three weeks after my arrival, the man of the family took me back to Broken Bow on the seat of his wagon. In the back was a large hog. "Ruth," he said, "the money from this hog is all I have to give you for saving my family." But his gratitude was pay enough. His family grew up and that five-year-old boy became a doctor. He came to see me one time after he had finished his education.

"You were always my inspiration in medical school," he said. "When my money ran out one time and it was difficult to stay in school, I thought of you and the flu epidemic."

Well, that hog money and that boy's gratitude was good pay, I felt!

I spent a year with my sister Lutie and her husband, George Sweeney, at the Camp Bird mine on the western slope of Colorado. The Una and Gertrude mines had been abandoned—in the Imogene Basin above Ouray, Colorado—in the early 1880s. In 1896 Tom Walsh, a friend of

George's, found some rich ore in his pyrite smelter at Ouray. He took up the claim next to the Gertrude and called it the Camp Bird.

Eventually he consolidated 103 mining claims and 12 mill sites, the whole operation covering more than 900 acres. In 1902 he sold out to some Englishmen. The Camp Bird holdings, as they were called, made one of the richest gold mines in the West.

George, Lutie, and I would stand in awe and watch the tram buckets come down with tons of gold ore in them. George was a watchman for the mines. Today, he would be called a security man, for he was trusted by Mr. Walsh and had a lot to do to prevent theft and arson. He took Lutie and me all over the area with him.

I never saw such lovely flowers, such beautiful scenery, and such a magnificent stream with its gorgeous water-falls. The Box Canyon at Ouray was a delightful place to picnic, and the tiny picture city of Ouray, squeezed in between two mountains, was wonderful to behold.

My friends who have traveled in the Swiss Alps tell me that the San Juan country of Colorado is the more beautiful of the two. We traveled by horseback or muleback to the mines—straight up, nine miles. There were some places where the poor old mules would crowd one another off into the abyss, and some people lost their lives on those mountain trails.

That was just part of what Aunt Babe told us that day. Her greatest pleasure now is to sit with family and friends and recount those experiences in the pioneer land of Nebraska in the 1880s and the wonders of Colorado's western slope in the 1890s. She maintains a wide correspondence with family members and friends, and no letter goes unanswered, although her blindness makes her writing difficult to read.

"Please write large with red pencil or crayon if possible," she urges her correspondents. "I can no longer read typewritten letters."

Aunt Babe seldom refers to her own good deeds, which are countless. She nursed the sick for many years—and cared for relatives often without any pay. She considered "taking care of sick friends" a privilege, not just a duty. And her friends have all been loyal and good to her. All her labors, so willingly shouldered throughout her long and active life, have provided her the inherent toughness to carry on, however difficult the road she has had to travel.

When World War II came, she was past seventy years of age. She had a most comfortable home with her sister, Hattie, one in which she was welcomed by both her sister and her sister's husband, Sam Tooley. (He had been the mayor of Broken Bow and later a state senator.)

But Aunt Babe felt that she must make some added contribution to the country in its time of need. So she went to California and worked in a factory where foodstuffs were prepared and processed for the armed forces! This work put her name on the Social Security records for the first time, and a check each month now comes in her mail box from this source.

She owns her own home, asks aid from no one, though she is appreciative of the smallest favors.

"And I still love gooseberry pie!" she says, her eyes twinkling.

As we left her standing on the porch, waving to us, following our last visit to her, a grandnephew who has known her since he was a baby, spoke up.

"You know, there's something actually *heroic* about Aunt Babe," he said warmly.

"Yes," one of the ladies in our party, a niece, spoke up, "and she's still *some woman*—even at ninety-five!"*

*Jennie Ruth (Aunt Babe) Chrisman, born 12 November 1872, died 27 March 1974 at Broken Bow, Nebraska. She was buried near her sisters and brothers in the Broken Bow Cemetery. Inscribed on her gravestone, together with her name and dates of birth and death is the honored title in the Chrisman family, "Aunt Babe."

11

Here They Killed Jed Smith

An attempt to pinpoint the exact location of Jedediah Smith's death site at the hands of Comanche Indians on the Cimarron River, 1831.

"JEDEDIAH S. SMITH"
He thought nothing in the works of God unworthy of his notice, and from constant observation he had amassed an immense fund of knowledge, exceedingly useful and interesting, in every branch of natural history. More than this, by his intimate knowledge of the geography of that immense tract of country, he had found that all the maps of it were full of errors, and worse than useless as guides to travelers.

Illinois Monthly Magazine,
June 1832

The exact location of the death site of Jedediah Strong Smith, pathfinder and explorer, "the greatest of the mountain men," as he was called by Jim Bridger, has never been established. Through the years the notion has grown that Smith died at or near the Lower Spring, later called Wagon Bed Spring, near the confluence of the Cimarron River's north and south forks, in what is today Grant County, Kansas, NW1/4 Sec. 33, Twp. 30 S. Range 37 W. This belief can be attributed to the fact that the Cimarron Cut-Off trail, which left the Arkansas River at the Cimarron crossing west of present Dodge City and struck almost a beeline for the two forks of the Cimarron River, became a popular route in wet years, after about 1825.

It was natural to assume that Smith must have been killed at the spring near the confluence of the Cimarron forks, since his wagon train of the year 1831 was attempting the hazardous crossing of the Cimarron desert, "El Jornado del Muerte," or "Journey of Death," as it was termed by the Mexican traders. That Smith might have died at another spring along the Cimarron was never considered, since his party did eventually reach the Wagon Bed Spring, referred to above, and later safely reached Santa Fe without further trouble.

Because of Smith's early death at thirty-two, and the fact that he never lived to record his great travels across the mountains and deserts of the West, his murder by Comanche Indians was unquestioned for many years. Only in recent years have historical facts and new insight, lent by the study of the old maps of that time, given credence to a statement once made by Smith's grandnephew,[1] Ezra Delos Smith, that Smith was killed about twenty to thirty miles down the Cimarron from the Wagon *Bed* Spring at another fine spring known to the Mexican traders as well as Indian tribes that traversed the region. This latter spring was early known as Wagon *Body* Spring, according to Jedediah's grandnephew, and "in our time," as the grandnephew put it, as Fargo Spring. In settlement days, Fargo Spring was named after a wealthy Chicago shoe manufacturer, C. H. Fargo, who owned land in the vicinity. Its location, as nearly as can be presently established (1962), is in Seward Precinct, 32-33-NW1/4, sec. 36, on the property of C. R. and R. L. Conover.

The naming of springs after "wagon bodies" and "wagon beds" came about as a natural part of the development of the West. Doubtless there are many more springs in the West so-named. The river sands near the springs along the Cimarron offered an ill-footing for both humans and animals in early times because of treacherous quicksands which bogged the animals. The customary practice, where rocks were available, was to throw in many rocks and brush around such springs, making a solid fill upon which the animals could tread with safety and assurance to the water hole to drink, for mules are notoriously careful of their footing. Carrying water in buckets fifty to a hundred feet to water livestock was a laborious process. Frequently, an old wagon bed that had been abandoned on the trail provided an excellent means for shoring up the banks of a spring and providing an area of containment, outside of which the earth and sand might be tramped down solidly to establish a solid footing at the spring.

The old wagon bed would be sunk into the soft sands over the spring, a hole knocked in its bottom with an axe to permit the water to rise into the box. The box would then be worked down into the sands with several men standing on it to a depth where less than a foot of the wagon bed would rim the spring. The earth around would be covered with dry sand, rocks, gravel, brush, or whatever was handy to provide a secure footing for the animals. The result was a veritable "water tank" in the ground.

By such means, both the spring at the confluence of the Cimarron forks, Wagon Bed Spring (called the "Lower Spring") and the big spring down river (later Fargo Spring) had been given their names, the latter being called by the early Santa Fe traders "Wagon *Body* Spring." It was not unusual to name springs after such occasions when the old wagon boxes were used, for as livestock gave out or were killed by Indians, or as the wagon wheels gave way, their tires worn out or running gears broken or lost, many such wagons were abandoned along the trails. They soon became firewood, caskets, grave markers—or spring walls—along the trails.

The origin of these "wagon body or wagon bed" springs is dealt with here somewhat in length, for it is through them the exact location of Jedediah Smith's death can be pinpointed.

Jedediah Strong Smith was born in 1799. He grew up in the wooded area of western New York State and northwestern Pennsylvania. His education came from his parents and from the tutelage of a neighbor, a Doctor Simons, who took an interest in him, providing him with the basic rudiments of an English education and a smattering of Latin. At the age of thirteen, young Smith was working in the Great Lakes trade. There he became aware of the vast, unexplored lands to the west of the Mississippi.

By 1818, at the age of nineteen, he had worked his way west as far as St. Louis. There he engaged with one of the very early American traders to make the trip westward to a rendezvous point where they would meet with Mexican traders from Santa Fe and exchange goods. The meeting was to be held on the international border at a point that would now be near present Dodge City, Kansas. That area south of the Arkansas, west of Dodge, was at that time Old Mexico.

When the American party reached the rendezvous, the Mexican traders had not shown up. After a wait, the American trader grew suspicious and turned back, deciding to trade his goods with Indians on the way back. His decision left the young man, Jed Smith, the choice of going on alone across dangerous and unknown trails to Santa Fe or returning with the American group. Smith was resolved not to return, and soon two companions agreed to accompany him to Santa Fe.

With the departure of the American party to the east, Smith and his companions crossed the Arkansas River and set out on horseback southwestward, down the old Indian trail that would eventually become called the Adobe Walls Trail.[2] Crossing Mulberry Creek, they came that night to a grassy, timbered, and well-watered spot where fine artesian springs fed into a stream flowing east by north. This location is near the large loop of Crooked Creek, north of present Meade, Kansas.

The following morning they continued on southwest, soon spying a cloud of dust before them that proved to be the Mexican company coming to the ill-timed rendezvous. Smith explained to the Mexicans that the American party had grown discouraged and departed for the east again. Thereupon the Mexican traders turned about and headed back to Santa Fe, Smith and his two companions accompanying them. That night they camped on the Cimarron, probably in the area where the later Adobe Walls Trail crossed the river in the neighborhood of the present Davies Ranch, or on what is known as "the McClure place," about fifteen miles downstream from "Fargo Spring."

The Cimarron River was at this time poorly charted on maps— actually only cartographic guesswork—and appeared as a wiggly line, always running in a due west-to-east line, with no indication of the great southeasterly drop of the river from its two forks.[3] However, on these early maps the "Osage Trail" through what is today the panhandle of Oklahoma was well charted and the course of the Beaver (North Canadian) River was amply shown to guide any party traveling from east to west or vice versa.

Doubtless, the return to Santa Fe by Smith and his newfound friends of the Mexican party was accomplished by passing westward after reaching the Beaver River, or after following the well-known Palo Duro Creek southwestward into what is today the Texas panhandle, the river and stream courses leading them unerringly to the vicinity of Las Vegas and Santa Fe. The point is that the crossing from the Arkansas to the Cimarron which Smith made in 1818, according to the statement of his grandnephew, Ezra Delos Smith, mentioned above, was made along the line of the later Adobe Walls Trail. It was not made in a crossing from the Cimarron Crossing to the two forks of the Cimarron, as has been generally accepted as the only "cut-across" route. (The story of this early Smith tour of exploration is told in the *Kansas Historical Quarterly Collections*, vol. 12, p. 252, where E. D. Smith relates this story as one coming from the lips of his grandfather, Ralph Smith, Jedediah Smith's brother.) Ralph Smith had heard it from Jed Smith presumably in the winter of 1821, "on the only visit made to his home after he came west."

Following his arrival in Santa Fe, Jedediah Smith is reported to have turned northward to Salt Lake,[4] then reached the upper waters of the Platte River, presumably the Sweetwater, near South Pass, which led him back to St. Louis the winter of 1819 or 1820. From that point, Smith made another trip to western Kansas and eastern Colorado, trapping and trading as far west as the Platte.

Most historians first pick up Jed Smith's trail when he answered an advertisement inserted in the *St. Louis (Mo.) Gazette and Public Advertiser*, 3 February 1822, calling for a hundred "enterprising young men" to ascend the Missouri River to its source, "there to be employed for one, two or three years." Smith, "who had passed the previous summer and fall in Illinois and Indiana" later recorded that he "found no difficulty in making a bargain on as good terms as I had reason to expect."

With Gen. W. H. Ashley and his party, Smith ascended the Missouri early in 1822 and explored in the Rocky Mountain region, returning to St. Louis in October of 1825 after becoming a partner of Ashley's. The years 1826 to 1828 Smith spent on California expeditions, in 1827 passing across the desert on his newly discovered route from Salt Lake to Los Angeles. These excursions were attended with great difficulties and disappointments, but have been so well recorded there is no reason to pursue them further here. The spring of 1828, Smith was in Oregon, trading with the Indians along the Columbia River. Here he again encountered great trouble, having his camp and all but three of his men wiped out, his goods stolen. Through the chief factor, McLoughlin, at Fort Vancouver, he recovered his trade goods, sold them to the factor, and returned to St. Louis by way of Wind River and the Powder River in Wyoming.

By this time Smith had entered into a partnership with Jackson and Sublette which he now broke up on his return to civilization. He had a keen desire to quit the fur trade, to record his extensive travels, and to chart on hand-drawn maps, at which he had become proficient, his distant travels across the mountains and deserts of the great western land.

But when he reached St. Louis he found there his two brothers, Peter and Austin, both eager to make a trading trip to Santa Fe. To accommodate them, Jed Smith commenced to outfit a train for Santa Fe, purchasing wagons, mule teams, and helping select and gather the trade goods. Jackson and Sublette now decided to join Smith again and between the three experienced traders they put together the largest and best-organized train yet to leave for Santa Fe. The wagon train consisted of twenty-three wagons, each drawn by six good mules, a party of eighty-three men. One wagon mounted a six-pound cannon on its rear wheels and carried a large chest of ammunition over its front running gears. One of the experienced mountain men, Thomas Fitzpatrick ("Broken Hand"), who had accompanied Smith on the Ashley expedition, soon joined the train after it had left the camp ten miles south of Independence, Missouri, on 4 May 1831.

The early part of the trip was without incident. The mule train made good time under the well-equipped teamsters, nearly all being experienced trail men. When they reached the Little Arkansas, one of Sublette's clerks, named Winter, went alone on the plain to kill a buffalo. A band of Pawnee braves waylaid and killed him. Within a few days after this tragedy the train reached the Cimarron Crossing of the Arkansas River. Here they were faced with the prospect of crossing a sixty-mile arid and flat plain, the trip known to Mexican traders as *El Jornado del Muerte*.

It was an extremely dry year, with no hope for the freshwater lakes made by the rains of a wet season to help them make the crossing as in wet years. Smith was well aware of the dangers of attempting the crossing along a route that had been plainly marked on the map drawn by the surveyor, Brown, two years before, "This route unsafe in very dry years." Smith had crossed that way before, had seen the prairie strewn with the skeletal remains of both men and beasts who found relief from the torturous trail only in death. So now calling up memories from the trip he had made in 1818 with the Mexican traders, he decided to try the other route, that of his 1818 trip to Santa Fe.

Immediately after crossing the Arkansas River at the "Semarone" Crossing, Smith ordered the lead teams to turn due south. He told the drivers that fifteen or twenty miles south they would come upon the several artesian springs that had served as a campground and watering place for the company with which he had traveled thirteen years before. Smith believed that southward they were bound to strike the Cimarron valley, for all maps he had seen at the time showed the Cimarron River flowing in a due easterly course from its two forks. On the map of the surveyor, Joseph C. Brown, drawn in the years 1825 to 1827, the Santa Fe Trail had been chartered from Fort Osage to Taos, but only that portion that Brown had traversed. As a result Brown's map, while showing the dangerous "dry route" sketched in lightly as a warning to travelers, brought the Cimarron River to an abrupt end just east of its forks, but left the feeling that its course continued on *directly eastward*, exactly as shown on all of the older maps. It was an extremely misleading map upon which to rely as to the river's actual course in the area. For with the normal drainage pattern lying west to east, what explorer or pathfinder would realize that the deceptive Cimarron, after flowing from its headwaters nearly a hundred and fifty miles to the *northeast* to effect its junction with the north fork would suddenly dip *southeastward* for a running distance of fifty miles, level off at what is today the Kansas-Oklahoma state line, then launch into another *southeastward* drop for a journey of another 140 miles? This was a factor Smith could not know or interpret from any existing map, yet he did know that when he had traveled south far enough he should reach the Cimarron valley, just as had been done when he crossed the prairie in 1818.

Smith's previous experience told him that southward from the

Arkansas, twenty miles or so, they would encounter the good small springs that fed the stream that flowed northeastward. All maps would have led him to believe that this stream, Crooked Creek, was the continuation of the Cimarron River from its forks. That evening late, the wagon train reached the site of the springs. The springs were dust-dry! Smith sent scouts east and west to look for flowing water. All reported only dry springs. The following morning a wider search was made. The reports came in, all springs were dry. Nor could they raise water by digging in the hot sands where the springs had once brought cold water to the surface.

Jed Smith realized the seriousness of their position. The river, he knew now, must be still farther to the south. But he knew the precarious position he would be in to move the wagon teams farther out onto the plain without some assurance of reaching water—and soon. Perhaps Smith's memory was faulty at this point; perhaps he recalled the journey of 1818 as a somewhat lesser journey than what lay before them. Perhaps the experienced Mexican traders and trail men with whom he had previously crossed the plains had taken a trail a few miles farther east than where Smith now found himself. This would have permitted them to travel down the main trunk of the stream now called Crooked Creek (then frequently mistaken for the Cimarron) on the trail that later became the Jones and Plummer Freight Trail. This trail crosses over the high land, leaving Crooked Creek at its eastward bend, crosses the Cimarron, and reaches the Beaver (North Canadian) River on the Osage Trail in an easy two-day trip for wagon teams. Whatever Smith's thoughts, his action was one of an experienced pathfinder. He called upon Tom Fitzpatrick and together the two men set off in a southerly direction to look for the Cimarron Valley.

That morning when Smith and Fitzpatrick left their camp, Smith gave the order to the wagon men to await their return before moving. When he and his companion had traveled south a few miles, Smith no doubt saw the opal haze that hangs over the Cimarron Valley in the early spring mornings and sent Fitzpatrick back to bring the wagon train up along their trail. Fitzpatrick's last sight of Smith was through his field glasses at a distance of several miles. Jed Smith was heading southwest. He was never seen again; nor was his body recovered.

The wagon train moved out according to Smith's instructions. A grass trail is difficult to follow even when a damp, early morning dew, with the sun's rays shining upon it from a low angle, is on the trail. Across dry, dusty buffalo grass it is almost impossible to follow a horse's trail. When Smith's "sign" could no longer be picked up, the wagon train halted. More scouts were sent out west and south to look for water. The train continued on uncertainly in a southwestward direction. Hours later one of the scouts returned. He had seen the Cimarron Valley—to the west! The next day the wagon train reached the Cimarron River, somewhat below its forks. Making their way upstream, the men camped at the "Lower Spring" a day and rested their teams and washed in its cool waters.

After sending Tom Fitzpatrick back to the wagon train, Smith had continued on southwestward. As he came closer to the Cimarron Valley he could detect it as a dark line of mist, the high plains on its far side looming up above the opalescent line to define the horizon. Continuing on for another hour he came to the head of a ravine that cut through the prairie sod, leading southward to a series of small canyons.[5] Down through these rough breaks he pushed his weary animal until he came to the place where the canyons opened out onto the Cimarron Valley. He soon came upon a fine, large spring of cool water only a few rods back from the banks of the river. Dismounting, he took the bit from the horse's mouth and permitted it to drink from the waters. Then he got down on his hands and knees and washed his face and drank deeply of the cold, sweet water. He had found the fine spring on the Cimarron banks. Soon the wagon train (he hoped) would follow him to its waters.

No one knows the exact manner of Jedediah's death, except to know that he was killed by Comanche Indians, apparently at this big spring, which was later to be called Fargo Spring. The balance of the wagon train reached Santa Fe on 4 July 1831. Jed's fate was learned later when Austin Smith purchased his brother's rifle and pistol from Mexican Comancheros who had traded with Comanche Indians for them. The Comanches, the Mexicans said, related to them how Jed had died at their hands. In September, that same year, from a point along the return trail, Austin Smith wrote his father of Jedediah's death. Faded and absent portions of the letter have been interpreted and inserted parenthetically by the writer and may, of course, be in error, but the letter is, otherwise, a true copy from the original.[6]

> Walnut Creek on the Arkansas
> 300 miles from the settlements
> of Mo.
> Sept. 24, 1831-

My Dear
    Farther [sic]

It is the [pain]ful [l]ot [at] times to con[vey] [a death statement] of a friend,—but [when it falls] to the lot of a son to communicate to a Farther the death of a Brother it is more so—Your son Jedediah was killed on the Semerone the 27th of May on his way to Santa Fe by the Curmanche Indians, his party was in distress for water and he had gone in search for the above river which he found when attacked by fifteen or twenty of them—they succeeded in alarming his animal, not daring to fire on him so long as they kept face to face. So soon as his horse turned they fired, and wounded him in the shoulder. He then fired his gun and killed their head chief. It is supposed they then *rushed* upon him and despatched him.

Such, my Farther is the fate of him you loved. I am convinced that this intelligence will grieve you much, but do not, my dear farther, take it to heart too sorely.

I left Santa Fe the 28th of August and Peter left the following day for California for the purpose of purchasing mules. I do not apprehend any danger in the trip, it is often made with 8 or ten men and no defeats or difficulties experienced. I shall be in St Louis along the first of November***

I am dear farther your son forever,

> Austin C. Smith

So died Jedediah Strong Smith, at a waterhole along the course of the Cimarron River. From the facts given above it may be seen that Smith was slain at some other spring on the Cimarron than the one known as the "Lower Spring," at the Cimarron forks, or later known as Wagon Bed Spring. For had he been slain at that location his party would have found his remains when they reached the spring!

Smith's grandnephew, Ezra D. Smith, Meade, Kansas, wrote in a letter (1915) mentioned in the *Kansas Historical Quarterly*, vol. 28, p. 185 that his great uncle died

> . . . at a water hole known in my time as Fargo Spring, to the later Santa Fe traders as Wagon *Body* Spring. Do not confuse this with Wagon *Bed* Spring just above the confluence of the Dry Cimarron with the Cimarron. This waterhole (Fargo Spring) was . . . on the north side of the Cimarron at the mouth of a canyon which comes down from the north, and is near the west line of Seward County, Kansas. . . .

The actual site of Fargo Spring is more nearly the center of Seward County than Ezra Smith thought. The old spring has been long since washed out by the great floods of 1908 and 1914, or filled in by erosion, according to some old pioneers. However, the location can be easily reached by driving north from Liberal, Kansas, on Highway U.S. 83, after crossing the Cimarron bridge on Highway 83, at its north end. Stop north of the bridge and search for the remains of the old Fargo schoolhouse. The Fargo Spring was southeast, on the river.

Since settlement days, about 1885, in Seward County, Kansas, this spring had retained its name of Fargo Spring, being named, as heretofore mentioned, after the wealthy Chicagoan, Fargo, who owned land nearby. The spring was near the earlier location of the Harwood Cattle Company's headquarters ranch. This outfit was managed by W. I. Harwood, whose post office was first at Dodge City and later "Harwoodville," which became, with the settling of the area, a town called Fargo Springs. Harwood's enterprise is listed in the *Brand Book of the Western Kansas Growers Association*, 7 April 1885, with the O Bar L Connected (Ⱡ) brand. His range is shown as "west of the 'Dobe Walls Trail" on the Cimarron. Fargo Springs, a new town in 1885, had died for all purposes by 1888 when the Chicago, Kansas, and Nebraska Railroad which built westward from Meade, Kansas, deflected southwest, crossed the Cimarron several miles below Fargo Springs, and turned southwest to pick up the Texas cattle business in the Neutral Strip.

Once the exact location of Jedediah Strong Smith's death at the hands of the Comanche Indians[7] can be established beyond a reasonable doubt, it would be most appropriate that the site be permanently marked to instruct future generations as to his character, personality, and heroic death. For Smith, it is becoming known, was one of the nation's greatest pathfinders, explorers, and trailblazers, to be compared favorably with other historical figures such as Jim Bridger, Father DeSmet, Meriwether Lewis, William Clark, Gen. W. H. Ashley, Kit Carson, David E. Jackson, W. L. Sublette—yes, and if you wish, such moderns as the astronauts Glenn, Shepard, and Armstrong! For he was certainly first on the scene in many geographical locations in the West, the Southwest, and the Northwest, opening the trails where others might follow him. Had he lived to record in words and with maps his great achievements, his name would already be honored with the greatest.

Later generations owe a debt of gratitude to Jed Smith, for many western cities have been built astride his trails and present arteries of commerce and transportation lie upon them. No one will ever recover his bones, but the site of his death at the big spring on the Cimarron banks should be marked in recognition of his deeds and to honor his name.

Notes

1. Ezra Delos Smith, "Jedediah S. Smith and the Settlement of Kansas," *Kansas Historical Quarterly Collections* vol. 12 (1915) pp. 252–53. A grandnephew of Jedediah Strong Smith and the son of his brother Ralph Smith, E. D. Smith wrote in 1914–15: "Much of my information came to me years ago by word of mouth, and consists of incidents related by Jedediah Smith to his brother Ralph on the only visit made to his home after he came west." This story of the first trip made overland by Jedediah Smith to Santa Fe is taken from E. D. Smith's writings.

The late Robert Evans, Liberal, Kansas, the son of pioneer stock and who lived near the old town of Fargo Springs in boyhood, located the old spring east one mile and a little north from the old town of Fargo Springs. "I am not positive this was the spring known as 'Fargo Spring' in my boyhood, but this was then and has always been my understanding. It was once on my father's land. It was a large free-flowing spring at that time." The author accompanied Mr. Evans to this location and, digging into sand, did locate a flow of water at a two-foot depth, following the heaviest rains (in June 1962) of eleven years.

Bernard Lemert, pioneer cattleman whose ranch lay just west of the town of Fargo Springs, placed the site of the "Fargo Spring" as south and east from the town, "just a few rods from the river." Charles E. Hancock, then eighty-nine, a Stevens and Seward county pioneer from 1885, also placed the Fargo Spring "on the lower ground, between the town and Gurney's Ranch." Though there were many "sand springs" along the river, the author accepts this location as the approximate location of the old Fargo (or Wagon *Body*) Spring at which Jedediah S. Smith met his death.

2. Harry E. Chrisman, *Lost Trails of the Cimarron* (Athens, Ohio: Swallow Press, 1964). The Adobe Walls Trail is therein charted on the end maps and can be noted as crossing the Cimarron River almost due east from Liberal, Kansas.

3. A. H. Brue's Map of 1833, in Morgan and Wheat, *Jedediah Smith and His Maps of the American West*, shows the "R. Semarone" as flowing west to east, paralleling the course of the Arkansas River. The Cimarron headwaters are shown as near those of the "R. Dolores," and with a short north fork and an extended south fork. This is the earliest map showing Smith influence, especially in the northwest areas.

Albert Gallatin's "Map of the Indian Tribes of North America," about 1600 A.D. along the Atlantic and about 1800 A.D. "westerly" (published in 1836), shows the Cimarron River flowing directly west to east, originating at the Spanish Peaks and again paralleling the course of the Arkansas River.

The David H. Burr Map of the U.S. of North America, 1839, shows the "Cimerone River" flowing *east by north* into the Arkansas River in the vicinity of present Dodge City. This map clearly shows the Osage Trail (or Road) through the Neutral Strip to Major Long's Creek. (Also see cut of section of the map published with House Report No. 474, 20 May 1834.)

All of the above maps would contribute to the contemporary belief that the Cimarron River's course was almost due west to east, paralleling the Arkansas River and in the one instance a tributary to that stream with the confluence near present Dodge City, Kansas, rather than (as is the true case) above Sand Springs, Oklahoma.

4. Smith's explorations at Salt Lake are not substantiated and would, in fact, deprive his friend Jim Bridger of its discovery should they be shown to have occurred. His trek across the area mentioned is supported only by his grandnephew's memory of the story as told him by Jedediah's brother, Ralph Smith. But such a trip, by a man of Smith's nerve, is not beyond the realm of possibility.

5. Smith struck the Cimarron River valley breaks about at the point where the town of Springfield (now deceased), Kansas, later stood. The ravine and small canyon which he followed south into the valley was the canyon where the sheriff of Seward County, Sam Dunn, was shot to death by a mob as a side issue resulting from the Hugoton-Woodsdale County Seat War in the late 1880s. The old buffalo trail, along which was laid the wagon road between Springfield and Fargo Springs, Kansas, was the trail followed by Smith when approaching the Cimarron River valley. See Smith, "Jedediah S. Smith."

6. Austin C. Smith, Letter from Kansas State Historical Society Archives.

7. As my research on the site of Jed Smith's death site progressed over several months, the idea kept recurring to me that it could have been the Mexicans (Comancheros), traders, *who actually killed Smith*. They were the ones who had Smith's weapons. All Austin C. Smith had was their word that Comanche Indians had killed Jedediah Smith. The well-experienced and trained Jed Smith, Indian-wise and careful, would have been much more easily "surprised" and slain by men he felt were friendly than by Comanche Indians whose traits he was well-acquainted with.

Bibliographical References

Hiram M. Chittenden, *The American Fur Trade of the Far West*. New York, 1902.

Dale L. Morgan, *Jedediah Smith and the Opening of the West*. Indianapolis: Bobbs-Merrill Co., 1953.

Dale L. Morgan and Carl I. Wheat. *Jedediah Smith and His Maps of the American West*. San Francisco: San Francisco Historical Society, 1954.

Maurice S. Sullivan. *Jedediah Smith, Trader and Trail Breaker*. New York: Press of The Pioneers, 1936.

The Trails of Jedediah Smith. A documentary outline including the journal of the great American pathfinder. Santa Ana, Calif: Fine Arts Press, 1934.

12

The Promised Painted Ponies

A stampede of 675 head of horses at Medicine Lodge causes Texas cattleman to break his word with his four sons.

The summer of 1878, Print Olive, the famous Nebraska cattleman, departed for Texas on a brief buying trip. Before leaving Plum Creek, now Lexington, Nebraska, he called his four sons to the large stable he had erected behind his fine town house. Billy, his oldest boy, was then eleven; Tom was nine, Harvey, seven, and little Al was just five years old. But eighty years later Al could recall the substance of the talk their father gave them, "just as though it had happened yesterday!"

The three older Olive boys were all good riders and Al, the youngest, was learning how to ride bareback, for the Olives never started a boy riding in the saddle. But the boys had only the cow horses to ride, animals their father kept in the Plum Creek town stable, for trips up to his range on the South Loup River.

The regular saddle horses were skittish, and broken in only for the roughest kind of trail and roundup work. Some of them, like Thunder, Old Banks, Billy The Kid (named after Olive's eldest son) and Blaze, were buckers at times, and dangerous for children to ride. Louisa, Print's wife, had stood fast for a change of riding animals for the boys. A dealer at Round Rock, Texas, had previously showed Print some Pinto stock, "painted ponies," as they called them, well-broke small-boned animals that would be excellent children's horses. Now Print told his sons about them.

"Boys, I'm bringing you back some painted ponies to ride. I'll get ten head of them, so you'll have a change each. Some of them will need training—maybe breaking—so you, Billy—and you, Tom—will have to work out the kinks. What do you say?"

The boys did a dance around their father, throwing their hats in the air and yipping like Cheyenne Indians at a scalp dance.

When the yelling subsided, their father spoke seriously.

"There's one provision that you all must satisfy. You must mind your mother and help her with her work. Agreed?" The boys nodded solemnly. "Alright," their father said, "I'll buy the ponies and they'll come up with the horse herd next spring from Texas. I'll have your Uncle Marion see that they get good care on the trip."

Print Olive kept his promise. He purchased the ponies and had them ready when the horse herd was gathered the following spring. But unforeseen troubles in Nebraska—the lynching of the two settlers Mitchell and Ketchum, who were stealing his cattle, his indictment for their murder, the celebrated criminal trial that followed in that spring of 1879, ending in his imprisonment—all these events diverted his attention from the painted ponies promised his sons.

The task fell to Ira W. Olive, Print's younger brother, to complete the plans for the delivery of the horses to Nebraska, and he made a trip to Texas early that spring. Ira Olive hired a friend, George M. Griffin, as the trail boss, since he could not make the long trip himself, now being shouldered with the responsibility of their Nebraska ranching enterprises. Griffin hired six men in addition to the younger Olive brother, Marion, to make the trip. These men were Arnold Armstrong, an Olive cowhand; Arnold's brother Tex; Jeanie Simmons, a neighbor boy; Martin L. Sides, another lad who had ridden for the Olives in Texas; Bob Van Zandt and his brother Lewis, both black men from Travis county, the latter to cook for the outfit; and one other man, known only as "Dock," and not too much trusted by Griffin and eventually discharged by him en route when trouble came to the outfit. Years later some men thought this character may have been the notorious Doc Middleton, the infamous horse thief who caused so much trouble on the central Nebraska range, but no proof was ever made for the case.

The horse herd was gathered at the Olive Pens, near present Thrall, Texas, and road-branded for the trip, the Olive horses wearing a large "O" hair brand on the hip, and Griffin's 100 head a small skin brand on the animals' jaws. The herd totaled 675 head, which included the 10 head of "painted ponies," promised to the sons of I. P. (Print) Olive, senior partner of the Olive Brothers livestock and ranching enterprises in Texas and Nebraska.

Following a brand and health inspection by John Henry Turner, the Williamson County inspector, the herd was turned out on the trail early in April. After an unruly day or two while the animals quieted down and worked off their nervousness, they joined the old Chisholm Trail at Belton and continued on north through Fort Worth, then the terminus of the Texas and Fort Worth railroad.

The herd crossed the Red River at the Red River Station, and entered the Indian Nations. The men were in good spirits, and their progress had been excellent. So good, in fact, that Griffin ordered a day's layover at the Red River Station to permit the younger animals time to rest and graze. There the men washed out their underclothes and socks and handkerchiefs, enjoyed a few belts from the ever-present bottle, and caught up on their sleep.

When the herd reached the area east of Turkey Creek on the Cimarron River, a few days later, Griffin decided to take the trail to the northwest and head for the Salt Fork of the Arkansas River. He could cut two days' time from his schedule by striking up the Gus Johnson Road to a point near the Salt Flats. The trail was plainly marked, he learned from a freight outfit hauling salt to the ranches, and few raids by Indians had taken place or were to be expected.

Griffin knew well what valued prizes the fine Steel Dust geldings and the ten head of painted ponies would be to raiding Indians, but he turned up Turkey Creek and toward the Medicine Lodge River in Kansas. Reaching the river, the herd crossed the Salt Fork south of the burgeoning town of Medicine Lodge and established their camp three miles east of the town on a wide prairie of fine grass.

For several days the drag and swing riders had been reporting the presence of Indians skulking along a half mile or a mile from the horse herd. Griffin, a cautious man, had been placing a double guard each night on the bedground.

Now north of the Kansas state line, and out of the Cherokee Strip, he felt somewhat safer from Indian raids. Nevertheless, he continued the double night guard at this camp where he planned to rest and graze the stock for two days, while on good grass, and with nearby water at the river.

That night Martin Sides rode up to the wagon with a report that he had seen nine Indians west of the herd, almost within the town limits of Medine Lodge. Griffin thought Sides must have seen some passing horsemen, so he paid little attention to the report. It was the first week in May, and the weather was excellent. It was a cool night, fine for sleeping. Now out of the Indian Nations, a false sense of security of the trail boss laid the ground for the tragedy that followed.

As the night waned, the big herd had been drawn together in a loose oval formation on the grassy bedground. The night was pitch black, with cloud cover, but all appeared to be peaceful and in good order in their camp. At two o'clock the trail boss, the Van Zandt brothers, and Tex Armstrong were asleep in their "little hot rolls" around the wagon, their night horses grazing nearby, tethered on stake ropes. It was customary in their camp for the night watch to ride slowly around the sleeping horses until meeting the other guard, then stop, exchange a few remarks, and continue on, usually whistling, singing, or humming some old song to assure the animals of their presence near the herd.

This night Marion Olive, Arnold Armstrong, Jeanie Simmons, and the man called Dock were out with the herd, since the doubled guard was just changing. Suddenly the men heard hoof beats to the west of the herd, and the popping of blankets, accompanied by shrill yelps and cries of Indians.

The big horse herd reacted as though a barrel of gunpowder had been exploded in its midst. Heads turned in all directions, the animals vanished from the bedground within a few seconds, the sound of their more than two thousand hooves on the hard prairie sod bringing up from the earth a sound like thunder as they scattered to the four winds, ears tucked tightly back, nostrils distended, and manes and tails whipping in the breeze. As the horse herd swept by and around them, the four men on night guard attempted to find the leaders of the stampede, but soon found themselves engulfed only in dust as the maddened animals dashed past them with the sound and fury of a Kansas cyclone.

Back at the wagon, Griffin and the cook were awakened by the roar of the hooves a half mile away and the sound of their own night horses tugging at the stake ropes. Hurriedly pulling on their boots, the trail boss and his remaining men took off after the fleeing horses, but they were now so badly scattered over the area and had such a lead that the men rode futilely back and forth, "too and fro" as Bob Van Zandt later described their search, but without locating a trace of the main herd, finding only scattered bunches of exhausted yearlings and two-year-olds.

By dawn a few of the men returned to the wagon for a cup of hot coffee, each bringing with him some of the horses until 250 head of the 675 horses in the herd were accounted for. Marion Olive, Arnold, and Dock were still out with the stampeded animals, wherever they might be. Later in the morning Jeanie Simmons rode in with a few of the better geldings and some mares, reporting that the main herd had struck back into Indian Territory, along the trail up which they had come, east of the Medicine Lodge River.

Griffin ordered the men to eat a good breakfast and take an hour's rest, then to be ready to travel again. He knew that either Indians of the Cheyenne or Arapaho tribes or white rustlers in the area had deliberately run the main herd south to the crossing of Driftwood Creek. From that point many of the horses had continued on down the old trail.

Significantly enough, the Steel Dust horses and the other mature geldings with better breeding had veered from the backtrail to the west and southwest, after crossing Driftwood. This meant one thing, Grifin reasoned, and that was that the Indians had taken their pick of the herd from the fleetest animals and headed them for their reservation lands in the Antelope Hills country. If white men, masquerading as Indians, as was frequently the case in this area, had been responsible for the stampede, Griffin realized that the animals would have been turned toward the Public Land Strip to the west, or "No Man's Land" as it was called, an ideal hideout for outlaws and thieves, and a land with no law or jails.

If the trail led into this strip, Griffin decided to wipe it from his schedule, for men like Dutch Henry and other outlaws could never be apprehended in that wild land. It would take determined lawmen, well-armed and ready to fight, to take the horses back from them. His few gun-shy cowboys and wranglers would be of little help.

The trail boss moved his temporary camp down from Kansas to a location on Eagle Chief Creek, on the T5 cattle range, to begin his search for the herd. Men of the T5, the Texas Land and Cattle Company, were all from Texas, and he knew his herd would be safe on their range while he took most of his men southwest to scour the Glass Mountain country and that region in the Antelope Hills. Only Marion Olive remained behind to watch out for the herd, while Griffin, accompanied by the wagon and his other men, set forth on their search.

The first day out the riders recovered two bands of horses containing thirty head each. The animals were held by Indians of the Cheyenne tribe, but were surrendered without trouble after Griffin counseled with their chief. Some of the animals had already been paint branded, others wore Indian burned brands. The manes and tails had been roached, and a few of the animals had their ears split at the top, Indian style. The animals now appeared as wild as the red men who had stolen them, but Griffin was glad to recover them without a fight. Later they picked up another 100 head.

Their search continued on for five weeks, making a total of six weeks of time lost, and in all those weary days they found only a few more head scattered among the hills, so Griffin decided to give up the hunt and return to the main herd at the big springs on Eagle Chief Creek.

After a day's rest the herd was again started up the trail. At Medicine Lodge, Griffin appointed a realtor, a Mr. McAllister, with the power of attorney to recover any more of the animals that could be found, for he was still short 195 head of Olive Brothers horses as well as 70 head of his own. As it eventually turned out, McAllister recovered another 40 head of the animals, but the final tally showed Olive Brothers 155 head short and Griffin took a loss of about 50 head. Very few of the fine Steel Dust geldings were recovered, and no trace was ever found of the 10 lovely painted ponies, the prize of the herd in the eyes of the Olive boys' father, and the little animals whose very mention afterward brought tears to the eyes of his four sons.

Print Olive probably never knew of the great disappointment his sons suffered at the loss of the painted ponies, for ironically enough, at that very time he was engaged in the greatest fight of his life—in fact a fight to save his life—in the district court at Hastings, in Adams County, Nebraska.

The previous fall of 1878 Print Olive and his cowboys had lynched the two settlers who had been stealing and butchering his beef and selling it at the Kearney market. In an attempt to bring the rustlers to justice, Bob Olive, another younger brother, had been appointed a deputy sheriff in Buffalo County, Nebraska, and was ordered to arrest the pair of thieves. In this attempt Bob died under the guns of the two cow rustlers. The murderers, Mitchell and Ketchum, later fell into Print Olive's hands when he offered a $700 reward for their arrest.

Once he had them, he promptly lynched the pair. Olive was indicted for their murder, and at the time of the Medicine Lodge stampede of his horse herd he was facing the gimlet-eyed Judge William Gaslin, a man who was determined to convict him. Engaged as he was in this fight for his life, Print Olive's attention had no doubt been averted from the matter of the painted ponies, which he had pormised to his sons. Olive was convicted of the murders, but was freed within two years by the Nebraska Supreme Court, which ruled that Judge Gaslin lacked the jurisdiction to try him in his Adams County court.

Now back at his South Loup ranch that winter of 1880-81, Print watched the great blizzards further decimate his once immense herds of livestock. Two years later he quit the Nebraska range and moved his family and remaining cattle to Kansas, where he established good ranches on the Smoky Hill River and Sawlog Creek, and a home in Dodge City.

In August 1886, I. P. Olive was shot to death in his own saloon at Trail City, Colorado, by a drunken cowboy, Joe Sparrow, who owed him a ten-dollar livery feed bill and other money.

Following Print's death, the Olive brothers' partnership was dissolved. The remaining brothers, Ira and Marion, could not work together. Marion went to the Blood Indian Reservation in Canada to work cattle and was never heard from again. Ira W. Olive became a banker and rancher at the town of Lexington, Nebraska. A shrewd and opportunistic man, Ira Olive seldom missed a chance to make money for himself and when he died in 1929 he was one of the richest men in the area. But it was about 1897 that Ira W. Olive learned that the U. S. Court of Claims had started making restitution for the theft claims due to Indian depredations in the old Cherokee Strip and Indian Nations.

The Indians were wards of the U.S. government, and this made the government responsible for their actions. So Ira W. Olive, together with George M. Griffin, the trail boss of the ill-fated horse herd of 1879, petitioned the U.S. Court of Claims for damages resulting from the stampede at Medine Lodge, Kansas, in 1879.

The case was numbered as Indian Depredations Case No. 9910, and was filed 31 May 1898. Griffin's claim was no. 9591 and was filed on the same date. By 1 August 1899, the testimony of Ira Olive, Griffin, and any other of their men that they could reach, was in the government's possession. On 5 December 1901, the government filed its cross-petition.

Time passed—the courts of the land were not noted for their alacrity in settling cases—and it was sixteen years later, in 1914, that the claims of both Ira Olive and of Griffin were disapproved, the Court of Claims denying that they had proven it was Indians who stampeded the herd! The court reasoned that it could have been white rustlers as well as Indians causing the trouble. Though eyewitnesses Bob Van Zandt, Martin Sides, and George Griffin all testified that they had seen Indians immediately prior to the stampede, the court ruled against them.

By this time Print Olive had been in his grave at Dodge City for twenty-eight years. His oldest son, Billy, had been gunned down on the streets of Beaver City, Oklahoma, twenty-seven years before. Tom, Harvey, and Al Olive were all now middle-aged men. The "promised painted ponies," as the family members had learned to speak of them, had now become only a nostalgic memory in their minds.

Al Olive, the last of the Olive men to die, passed away on 19 May 1960, at the age of eighty-six. But the memory of the promised painted poinies had remained with him throughout his long life. In the late 1950s, the writer was making a tape recording of an interview with him at Dodge City. At that time Al expressed his grief at what the thought must have been his father's disappointment over his failure, through no fault of his own, to keep his promise to his sons and deliver the little Pinto ponies to them.

"You know, Harry," he said at that time, "I have always grieved over them painted ponies—not so much because we boys didn't get them as because father couldn't keep his promise to us. Oh, we always had horses to ride, plenty of 'em. But I have always knowed how that must have hurt father."

I explained to Al that his regrets probably had little basis in fact, for his father's attention was no doubt called to those other and more important things at the time.

"Father was like all them old-time Texas cowmen," Al said. "They all believed in paying their debts, and their word was their bond. No, mother always said it hurt father most of all when he couldn't keep his word to us boys and bring back the promised painted ponies them Injuns ran off down in the strip."

So the thought of those lovely little spotted horses, their manes and tails roached, ears split at the top, and wearing painted symbols that were comprehensible only to the scowling young Cheyennes and Arapahos who straddled them, continued to fret and haunt the Olive family members, right down to this last son, three-quarters of a century after the stampede at Medicine Lodge.

13

Saga of an Indian Fighter, Captain James H. Cook

Recollections of Captain Cook, his son Harold, and their ranch at Agate Springs, on the Niobrara River in Nebraska.

My first meeting with Capt. James H. Cook was in the fall of 1921 or 1922, when my brother Hugh and I stayed overnight at Agate Springs ranch on the Niobrara River in the Nebraska Panhandle. We were moving a bunch of big mules for shipment at Mitchell, Nebraska, from summer pasture, southwest of Fort Robinson, on White River. We had made a late start that morning and reached Agate Springs ranch in midafternoon. I rode ahead to make arrangements for the night while Hugh held the mules a quarter of a mile north of the ranch.

As I dismounted in the yard Captain Cook, then in his early sixties but ramrod straight and with the appearance of a man of forty-five or fifty, came from the corrals leading his saddle horse. He was dressed in rough woolen clothes, worn boots, a kerchief around his throat, and with a light-colored western felt hat on his head. Only his graying hair and gray mustache revealed his years. I introduced myself and we shook hands. In the western manner, he began making preparations for our comfort at once.

"You can put your mules in the river pasture," he said, indicating a wire gate north of the ranch through which we could drive them. "There's plenty of grass and water."

The captain's friendly manner at once set me at ease and I signaled Hugh with my hat to bring the mules along. There were fifty or sixty head in the bunch and Captain Cook and I both walked out leading our horses, and helped turn them through the gate. As Hugh led, we followed along behind until the mules found the water where they began drinking, with the usual quarreling and kicking that is customary among these hybrids. At the captain's suggestion we watched while the mules watered at the river. He had trailed mules and worked them in the Southwest, he said, and never tired of their antics. As he watched them he appraised them and hoped our father would find a good market for them, for it was at a time when livestock was a burden and prices at a really low ebb. (As I recall today, those mules were shipped to North Carolina and lost father quite a bit of money.)

After a good hot supper we were shown our room upstairs in Captain Cook's fine ranch home and we retired early. At 4 o'clock in the morning we arose as quietly as possible so that we would not awaken the Cooks and fed our saddle horses. However, as we waited for them to eat Captain Cook appeared, inviting us to breakfast. Over bacon and eggs, oatmeal and black coffee, Hugh asked Captain Cook how much we owed him for the pasturage on the livestock and our night's lodging.

"Oh, about twenty dollars," the captain said with twinkling eyes and a broad smile. "That is payable in gold!" We realized that true western hospitality and manners still lived in this rather remote area, for his statement was, of course, a joke, and he would not take a cent for his favors as our host.

The captain and one of his men "helped start us out," as he termed it, and by high sunup we were well on our way. For many years afterward, when I had learned who Captain Cook was and found out about his frontier background, I grieved that because of my youthful ignorance I had not been able to take advantage of my brief visit with this amazing old Indian fighter, scout, big game hunter, Texas trail driver, and paleontologist. However, on this first visit I was but a boy of fifteen or sixteen years, new to that section of the country and with absolutely no knowledge of Captain Cook or his background. My brother, Hugh, though two years my senior, was as unequipped as I to take advantage of the moment, and both of us were far more interested in getting the long mule drive over with than in visiting with ranchmen along the way.

By the next time I saw Captain James H. Cook, twelve years later, I had read his great book *Fifty Years on the Old Frontier* and many other articles of an historical nature he had written for periodicals and newspapers, so I was prepared to visit with him and to appreciate his adventurous background and enjoy his many sterling qualities.

The year was 1933. That spring I had returned to the Nebraska Panhandle after three years in the Dakotas. In those intervening years, between my first meeting with Captain Cook and that day, I had hoped for an opportunity to again talk with him. That spring, as soon as the snow was clear from the ground, my fiancée, Catherine Bell, and a mutual friend of ours, Mr. Riley of the Nash-Finch Company, drove on a chilly morning to the Agage Springs ranch. We arrived shortly after noon and were served sandwiches and apple cobbler, the family having already eaten. Dr. Harold Cook, the captain's son, who had become a nationally known figure in archaeology and paleontology circles, was present, together with his charming wife, Margaret C. Cook. Dr. Cook was later with the Denver Museum of Natural History, which houses some of the Cooks' magnificent fossil specimens.

We were made comfortable in the large front room of the ranch home and discussed many subjects that were of general interest to all of us—the range cattle industry, Indian wars, the great fossil discoveries that Captain Cook and Harold Cook had made recently in the two nearby fossil beds, University Hill and Carnegie Hill. Eastern universities were, at this time, digging in those hills and further investigating the many fossil specimens contained in the matrices of the rocks.

The Agate Springs ranch house was warm and inviting, with the spring sun streaming in through the windows. There was a museum quality about the place that kept my eyes wandering from one wall to another where artifacts and relics gathered through the years by Captain Cook and his son were hung. Over the captain's desk, where he had written his historical articles and books, several of his old hunting rifles rested in a gun rack. A pair of beautifully beaded moccasins hung from a rawhide thong on a nail, a gift from Two Lance, an Ogalala Sioux friend. There were arrow shafts, many photos of old Indian friends such as Chief Red Cloud, Jack Red Cloud, his son, and Little Crow, who lived more than a hundred years. One particularly interesting article that held an unassuming position on the wall was a communication from his friend Charles M. Russell, the cowboy artist, a beautiful watercolor sketch in the Russell manner along with a letter to a friend from a friend who "would rather draw than write."

Captain Cook's remarks followed, I noticed, the wishes on the part of his guests. When the talk veered toward fossil discoveries and away from ranching and hunting, Cook unassumingly deferred to his learned son, yet I observed that when questioned directly about matters of a paleontological nature he spoke with great wisdom for he had devoted many years to the lay study of prehistoric times and their reptile-animal-bird life.

Captain James H. Cook was born 26 August 1857, in Michigan, the great-great-grandson of the famous English explorer and navigator, James Cook. Cook's father, Captain Henry Cook, was a seafaring man, and the lad's mother had died when the son was but two years old. Young Cook grew up in the home of the Titus family, friends of his father. Mr. Titus taught James Cook all the skills of the rifle and woodcraft that were common to the Michigan pioneers. Mrs. Titus brought the boy up as her own son, instilling in him the many Christian virtues possessed by the Titus family. Although Cook had the highest affection for the Titus people, his adventurous blood drove him to the frontier in the early 1870s and he went first to Kansas where he began to punch cows, then to Texas to become a "brush-popper," bringing the longhorns from the mesquite and cactus and fitting and taming them for the long trail north to the railheads of that day.

Cook learned fast and was soon a respected waddie in the employ of Ben Slaughter. A dogwood arrow, driven into the calf of his leg by a Lipan Indian changed the course of his career and he was soon driving cattle up the Chisholm Trail, meeting and working with such cowmen and pioneer Indian fighters as Dick Head and Major Frank North. Over the years he met and became friends with many Indians such as Chief Red Cloud, American Horse, and Young-Man-Afraid-of-His-Horses.

Between cattle drives, Cook had visited famous old Fort Laramie and hunted in Wyoming. He met and made friends for a lifetime with Army scout Baptiste ("Little Bat") Garnier. Cook's greatest desire was to become a successful hunter and trapper but, as he expressed it, "some invisible fetter" kept him bound to the life of a brush-popping Texas trail driver until 1878. That year, at Cheyenne, Wyoming, he made the break away from trail driving to that of big game hunter, taking a month's vacation during which he hunted and fished in the mountains of Wyoming and Colorado.

When Cook's vacation was over, he did not relish returning to Texas and the cattle trails, so he secured employment with "Wild Horse" Charlie Alexander, a mustanger turned hunter. Wild Horse Charlie was furnishing the Cheyenne butcher shops with antelope meat. Purchasing a Sharps .40-90, young Cook was ready for business.

The two men profited by hunting in the Crow Creek area, southeast of Cheyenne. They received between six and eight cents a pound for the meat, sold the dry hides at sixteen to twenty-five cents a pound. Soon Cook was engaged in hunting for the Union Pacific Railroad hotels with another companion, Billy Martin. Their hunting took them into the rugged mountain areas for elk, deer, and bear as well as the antelope on the plains. During this period, James H. Cook earned and saved $10,000, a considerable sum of money in those days. Since he neither drank nor cared for the "wild life" of the towns of that time, he laid his plans well toward eventual ownership of a good ranch for himself and his family.

In his extra work as a guide for eastern hunters, he came into contact with men whose influence was to change the course of his life. They were such scholars and scientists as Professors Cope, Marsh, Hayden, King, and others. Jim Cook had always been aware of his own inadequate education, yet he was a young man with an extremely keen mind and the inner desire to improve it. To do so, he told himself, he would need to keep company with those who had received good educations, men of competence and mental achievement. So it was not unusual that he deliberately sought out the company of these types of gentlemen and scholars, even though his work kept him far away from the centers of education.

Among some of the men he met were three Englishmen who were preparing to purchase ranch properties in New Mexico. Singling Cook out as a competent young man with the qualities they needed and with the experience to help them in their choice, they engaged his services. He accompanied them to the southwestern part of New Mexico, where he helped them select their ranch properties near the Mogollon Mountains. Mr. Harold Wilson, one of the Englishmen, hired Cook to manage his ranch which Cook did until the year 1887. This was the famous WS ranch, about eighty miles northwest of Silver City. Here, Cook felt he was truly on the western frontier, and to the song, "The Texas Lullaby," which he had learned along the cattle trails, he now added a new verse:

> Way up high in the Mokiones,
>   among the mountain tops,
> a lion cleaned a yearlin's bones,
>   and licked his thankful chops.

During the period Cook was manager of the WS, the great Apache chieftain, Geronimo, and some of his braves broke away from the reservation and fled to mountain retreats, leaving behind them a trail of depredations and murders. Cook and his ranch cowboys took the trail after the Indians, soon meeting up with Lt. Charles B. Gatewood and troopers of the Sixth Cavalry who were scouting for Captain Allen Smith commanding a few troops of the Eighth Cavalry, together with some Apache scouts. Cook had several sharp encounters with remnants of Geronimo's band, but never came into direct conflict with the main body of Geronimo's warriors, who fled and escaped into Old Mexico. When Cook left New Mexico, he had earned the title "Captain" Cook, by which most of his friends and acquaintances thereafter called him, and the U.S. government issued a bronze medal to him in consideration of his valued services to the army as scout and guide in the Apache troubles.

Cook returned to Cheyenne in 1887. He had married Katie Graham, daughter of Dr. E. B. Graham who owned a fine ranch on the Niobrara River in the Nebraska Panhandle, one of the first ranches of that section of the old Sioux hunting grounds. The ranch was known as the O Bar 4. Cook was now a mature man with the background of a successful ranch manager, an excellent judge of livestock, experienced and capable. He had now been hunting on the frontier, trail driving, and ranching for many years and had become a man of broad human sympathies and great understanding, one who had seen human beings at both their worst and best. His life had been enriched by many dramatic incidents and adventures. These episodes in which he had made many narrow escapes from both physical injury and death had taught him to regard all life as precious, and he had built within himself the alertness and the awareness necessary for survival on the plains. Cook had witnessed the manner in which Indians had been driven from their home grounds, and how their orderly tribal laws had been replaced by an alien law they neither understood nor respected. Cook, being the perceptive man he was, had a deep sympathy for the American Indians and their tragic plight. So when his father-in-law, Dr. Graham, suggested that he purchase the O Bar 4 ranch and take his bride there to live, it was understandable that the nearby Sioux from the Pine Ridge were soon visiting with him and his wife at their new home.

Cook renamed his spread the Agate Springs ranch, after the lovely springs at the ranch that help make up the waters of the Niobrara River. In his earlier years Captain Cook had learned to speak the Sioux language well enough to get along in the normal conversations with Indian friends, but he was a master at "sign," the language of the hands as used over the plains. Now when the Indians pitched their tepees in his ranch yard he counseled long and wisely with them about the "fork-tongued" white men who had stolen their birthright and heritage. Cook always used great diplomacy when dealing with his Indian friends, counseling them against taking up the hatchet and tomahawk however grossly they had been deceived and treated on the reservations. His friendship with Red Cloud had now endured since 1875 and he had known Little Wound, Young-Man-Afraid-Of-His-Horses, and American Horse for many years, cherishing their friendship.

At these councils held there at his ranch on the Niobrara, Cook would always kill a beef and "spread out the blanket" of welcome for his guests. Through Cook's intercession for them, Red Cloud agreed, after several councils, to permit Prof. O. C. Marsh and others of the Smithsonion Institution and of Yale University to dig for fossils on Sioux treaty lands. The old chief had believed that whites wanted to dig only for gold, a sound and logical supposition after what had happened in the Black Hills.

127

In the autumn and winter of 1890–91 the Messiah craze broke out among the frustrated Indians in the West. When it came to the Sioux they began the Ghost Dance, the ritual which they believed would return their lands to them, bring back the buffalo, and end the white's regimentation and tyranny. Cook was invited to meet with Indian friends at the home of his old comrade, the scout Little Bat Garnier, at Fort Robinson. To the Indians' question whether they could and should dance the Ghost Dance despite the Indian agent's ruling against it, Captain Cook counseled them wisely.

"You should be permitted the Ghost Dance as long as you wish and you do not bring violence to others. But you should not dance it so long that you injure your own health and cloud your minds. The Great Spirit will bring about such changes as he wills, whether you do the Ghost Dance or not. And He will make His changes as He desires to do, whether the white man or the Indian likes it. All peoples have their own form of dancing, and they should be permitted to perform, each in his own fashion."

Little Bat told Cook that he felt if the Indians were permitted to do the Ghost Dance they would wear themselves out, exhaust themselves, and become free of their anxieties. The Indian agent, Royer, however, felt differently and continued to halt the dances. This brought further anger on the part of the Sioux.

The strained relationship at the time of the surrender of Big Foot's band, and the tragic aftermath, called the Battle of Wounded Knee, is well-known history. Captain Cook was present at the time of the hostilities, but retained the respect of the Indians, for whom he held the greatest sympathy.

In the years that followed the tragedy of Wounded Knee and the useless slaughter of many peaceful Indians, many of the survivors came annually to Agate Springs ranch to visit Captain Cook. They brought gifts of beautiful bead work and leather items. One subchief's wife brought a lovely little wooden bowl which had a head carved upon it and she presented this valued family posession to him.

"She told me her father captured it after the burning of a wagon train in the Platte Valley," Captain Cook related. "All else was destroyed. But the Indians feared the image carved on the little bowl. They reasoned it might be the white man's God, and could cause the

Indians great trouble if it was destroyed by fire. So the warrior brought it back, and his wife used it at the fireside. It accompanied the tribe wherever they hunted, fought and traveled."

In one room of the museum in the ranch home, suspended from the ceiling, was a well-tanned cowhide, or it could have been a buffalo hide. In 1909 two of the old Sioux warriors who had helped defeat General Custer at the Little Bighorn came by invitation to Agate Springs ranch where they were to retell their story of the battle. An Indian artist came with them, and as they related their stories of the defeat of Custer's Seventh Cavalry and guided him, the artist put down in pictograph form on the tanned hide the story they related. Chief Red Cloud was present part of the time while their story was being unfolded and painted on the hide.

These pictographs tell the Sioux side of the Battle of the Little Big Horn. In relating some of the stories of this battle, Captain Cook said, the Indians held the viewpoint that there was no great "battle," for when the Indians charged, Custer's command was dismounted and scattered in five minutes before the great numbers of Indians who set upon them. Only eight Indians were killed. Custer was among the first wounded, and Knife Chief, a Sioux subchief, covered Custer with a blanket, hoping to take him prisoner. But a Sioux woman found the badly wounded officer and killed him with her skinning knife. The story may be apocryphal, or it may be told by the Indians only to further degrade and shame the Custer image and retaliate for the slaughter of women and children of their tribes at such other far-flung Indian battlefields as the Washita and Sand Creek. Today, the once-brilliant colors on the painted hide are fading, and the story it told, never too clear even to the Cooks, father and son, grows even dimmer. Yet it is a truly wonderful piece of Indian art in the best sense— dramatic, meaningful, and colorful in its primitive style.

Captain Cook and Harold Cook both took great pleasure in showing this rich collection to all interested folks who visited their home, and that was not a few, since he estimated at the time of our 1933 visit that about 5,000 persons passed through the museum-home annually. I am certain that number grew and doubled as others learned, like myself, about this interesting man, his brilliant son, and charming daughter-in-law.

129

Upon the death of Captain Cook in 1942, his fond hope that Agate Springs ranch might be devoted to the education and entertainment of thousands more Americans interested in the Old West was realized and became the life work of his son and daughter-in-law, Margaret C. Cook. When Dr. Harold Cook died in 1962, his wife continued the work. Both his father and Harold had wanted to make the ranch a gift to the United States government as a national park area with the museum collections and the fossil hills to be made available to all Americans. A bill was drafted and presented in Congress, giving a four-mile stretch of the rich Niobrara Valley, two or more miles in width, to the United States to be set aside as the Agate Fossil Beds National Monument. The bill was passed in June 1965.

That lovely area lies between Mitchell and Harrison, Nebraska, on a good hard-surfaced highway, No. 29, making the Agate Springs Ranch available to all, and certainly a worthy place to visit while en route to or from Yellowstone Park, Fort Laramie, Fort Robinson, Scotts Bluff National Monument, Glacier National Park, and other recreation areas in the North and Northwest.

The magnificent Cook collection is now in storage and will be taken out when the visitor center is ready for it. The museum over the quarries will be a magnificent thing, second only in the world, and similar to the Dinosaur National Monument. It is also hoped that a research center of paleontology with Dr. Harold Cook's scientific library as a nucleus may eventually be established there where lectures, slides, and movies may reach the general public during visits to the Agate Springs locale.

Though visitors who will never meet Captain James H. Cook in person will miss much, there are many relics and artifacts he collected to be placed in the showcases and on the walls that will help tell his own story of his life on the frontier. I shall always remember the gracefulness of his hands as he spoke, and specifically when he last said goodbye to us in the Agate Springs ranch yard, demonstrating the fashion of the Plains Indians' farewell signs.

The thought came to me that day that a sweeter and perhaps better age had passed beyond recall and that I was receiving her farewell caresses through the agile and expressive hands of one of her very last Sign Talkers.

14

George Phippen, Western Artist (1916–1966)

A tribute to one of America's great western artists, the late
George Phippen of Arizona.

It was a great satisfaction to the myriad admirers of the late, great
artist, George Phippen, that his true worth was recognized before his
premature death. He was a master of elegance in his sculptured
pieces, and an exponent of bold, glowing color in his paintings. His
respect for the western subjects he painted and molded was such that
historical accuracy was a creed.

George's official career as an artist, which began in 1946, came
suddenly to a tragic end on 13 April 1966, when he died of cancer.
This talented man was fifty years old, an age when another artist of
comparable talent, Charles M. Russell, was beginning to produce
some of his greatest work. Unofficially, George's artistic creativity
had been in play since childhood, for he could not recall a time when
he was not "sketchin' with the chewed stub of a pencil or modeling
with the red clay from a nearby creek bank."

George Phippen was born in Iowa, at Charles City. He moved, at a
tender age, with his family to Kansas, and there on a small ranch
George learned to ride horseback, build a loop for a lariat, herd cattle
out of the cornfields, and work the big teams of draft horses. Of all the
farm animals, the saddle horses and the cattle appealed most to him,
and they soon became favorite subjects for his sketches and his clay
models.

By the time George turned sixteen, he had begun to associate
himself with some form of art as a means of self-expression. For his

hands could not keep from sketching and modeling that which his eyes found beautiful and his imaginative mind found interesting.

When the Great Depression lay over the land, George, with thousands of other young men, found himself in a Civilian Conservation Corps (CCC) camp in the Minnesota lake country, working in the forests and along the lake shores. The majesty of this pristine land deeply impressed young George and turned him to color painting in the attempt to portray the dazzling landscapes.

Hardly had the CCC period ended when George was caught up in World War II. Though he always laughed at his five long years in the service as a coast guardsman on a single base in Washington State, it is well to remember that in wars "he also serves who only stands and waits." George, along with many others who wanted to get along with their lives at this time, found military life oppressive and unproductive. But he also found good fortune at that time because at Walla Walla, he met Louise Goble, a pretty coed with thoughts of a career. Louise and George were married in 1941.

Following his honorable discharge from the service, the Phippins established their home at Santa Fe, New Mexico, where George received good advice from other artists and studied the art techniques they employed. But soon George became uneasy, what with a growing family to support and no steady income-producing job. It was at this time that Louise stepped in with advice that proved to be the best her husband had ever received.

"She told me that my job was to paint," George recalled many years later. "As long as we have two months' groceries on the shelves, you will continue to study and work at your art," was Louise's ruling.

George grudgingly accepted her terms, though with some misgivings. "She kept assuring me that I had talent, that I was something different. I guess I owe about everything to Louise." George recalled of that point in his life.

The family was increasing, eventually to reach four sons—Ernie, Loren, Darrel, and Lynn—and one daughter—Winona.

Like most men who have known hardships and loneliness in youth, George, who spent many years on farms and ranches, in logging camps and military barracks, cherished most of all his loving wife and children. He wanted a ranchette for himself and his growing family, and he had always liked Arizona, so he moved to Prescott, where he could be in "cow-country" to work on his western scenes. There his genius flowered. With the exception of a two-year period spent in western Colorado, the Phippen family have lived in Arizona ever since. There, in magnificent oil paints and bronzes, George eventually found himself able to produce the outward manifestations of his artistic inner vision.

My friendship with George Phippen dates back to a day when I first saw an oil painting which he executed in the early 1950s. I instantly recognized the tremendous power and beauty of his work and wrote him in complimentary terms. In my letter I stated some personal preferences in western painting and sculpture. That started an inter-mittent correspondence that was carried on for more than fifteen years. Our first opportunity to meet came in 1964, when my wife and I were returning from a California trip.

At Ash Fork, Arizona, on famous Highway 66, we studied the road map. Prescott was barely fifty miles south; Skull Valley, and George's Lone Burro Ranch, a dozen or so more miles. We spotted a telephone booth alongside the highway and I called the Phippens. Louise answered. George was away but would be back by the time we arrived. "Come on down, you two," Louise invited in her friendly manner, "we both want to meet you."

The Phippen ranch home was exactly what one would have ex-pected. It was homey, comfortable, but without ostentation in any form. Louise was as charming as our conversation had indicated she would be. But George, when he arrived, was a surprise to me. Where I had always associated him, in my mind, with the rough-and-ready characters he depicted in his western paintings and sculpture, I found instead a man of great sensitivity. Shy—a truly "gentle" man, as my wife later described him. Not that George didn't love the rough life in the roping corral or on the roundup; it was simply that his innate modesty made him shy and retiring.

George Phippen was a man of great personal warmth, I soon found, and since I had always considered him somewhat of a kindred soul in our correspondence, I was now pleased to find him friendly, easy to talk with, and with a manner that instantly attracted others to him.

We had promised Louise we would take less than an hour of George's time, but as one hour passed, then another, we were all so busy talking, comparing, laughing, that several hours passed by without notice.

We had gone to the Phippens hoping to see much more of his art, but we soon learned that his work didn't stay long in his studio once he had signed it with the familiar "Geo. Phippen," and his famous earmarks. Only one painting, a lovely western snow scene, hung over the fireplace—and it had been sold to Earl Ford, we learned, but was yet undelivered!

I was reminded of a statement George made in a letter he had written several years before.

> As for Time on my part, I can't even find time to work my colts any more. I'm getting busier, and Old Dad Time isn't making my brush move any faster. Seems I don't get any letters answered, and worst of all I don't even get my Thank You notes written. But I just figure that everyone realizes that I do thank them for every kindness. The art game is something different than the usual run of business. In most fields, generally speaking, one can hire several others to work for you. Me, I have three or four times as much as I can do alone. . . .

On another occasion George had lamented:

> A painter rides a different saddle than businessmen. Others can hire help when they get stampeded with work. A painter or sculptor just has to stretch out his hours and do the best he can with what time he can steal from himself.

By stretching out his hours, sometimes to twelve and fifteen hours a day, George Phippen produced more than fifty celebrated oil paintings, all of which have been snatched up by private collectors and museums of fine art over the country. His paintings bring from $20,000 to $50,000 each. He produced hundreds of pen and ink sketches and watercolors, and a few magnificent sculptures cast in bronze that are the pride of every museum or individual that owns one.

The road to national recognition never came easy for George. Working at a distance from the historical epoch that produced Russell and Remington, Phippen's first efforts were ignored by careless critics as "imitations" of Russell's and Remington's works. A few called his paintings "illustrations," just as some forgotten critics once called Charles M. Russell an "illustrator." Of course they were wrong, as many since have confessed.

True, Phippen's work is in the manner of all famous western action artists of the past—honestly done, telling a rich story of that era with simplicity. Any viewer of his work—man, woman, or child—can understand and appreciate it. It needs no sophisticated interpretation.

Phippen worked often in the humorous style that is associated with natural western life on the frontier. But if there is any word that truly defines the art of George Phippen, and is indicative of the man himself, that word is *integrity*. Every piece of art he completed bears the stamp of his personal integrity as a full-fledged, if self-taught, artist of the first rank. Each piece is distinctly original, with indefatigable research to enrich it, and is historically and artistically unimpeachable as fine, western American art.

As a result of his researches prior to launching on a new creation, in oil, watercolor, or bronze, Phippen could discourse with experts upon many complex historical subjects and leave them with fresh material to think about. His bronze, *Padre Kino*, has all the force and tenderness of great art. The Jesuit missionary of northern Sonora and Arizona is depicted (about 1687–1711) atop a rocky desert elevation gazing into the misty distance, his faithful Indian aide and guide squatting at the missionary's feet. The padre holds a protective and comforting arm around the shoulders of an Indian child. The bronze exudes the humanity of the brilliant Kino and his feeling for the hungry and the oppressed.

Mountain Man, another stately bronze, depicts one of Bridger's or Carson's men intently scanning the area for signs of danger, yet the statue mystically shows all the rugged strength of the Rocky Mountains in this man seated on his faithful mule. *Apache* shows a wary

Indian on his pony climbing a rocky slope. There is all the furtive feeling of a hunted being in this magnificent piece.

For several years George produced western calendar art for a nationally known company. During this period he completed many worthwhile oils. Yet it was not a particularly happy period for him; the work was without challenge to his artistic being because company officials would suggest composition and color effects to better harmonize with the lithographic processes. It was not to Phippen's liking to paint as others directed.

George was a perfectionist in every respect and yet, during this "calendar art" period he happily produced some fine works, such as *Headin' 'em Off,* a painting that had greater calendar sales than any other western calendar had enjoyed and which ranked as tenth bestseller for the company!

Phippen's perfectionism paid off. When bronze-casting facilities failed to meet his own critical requirements, he searched about to improve the casting and with a friend set up his own foundry to mold his bronzes to the fine style on which he insisted. As a result, his bronzes were superbly cast. Ed H. Honnen, Denver businessman and art fancier, owns many Russell bronzes—has two *Will Rogers*—and most of Phippen's bronzes. He regards Phippen's work as superior to that of the great Montanan, blaming, most certainly, the poor quality of the casting of most of Charles Russell's sculptures.

Olive Trail Herd, has fine composition and the bold color that is the Phippen hallmark. His research for this painting included personnel, clothing, weapons, livestock, terrain, and all saddle gear.

Critics who cast a questioning eye on Phippen's basic research were always due for a surprise. One art buyer told the writer how he had commissioned George to do the figure of a buffalo in bronze. When George showed him the initial model in clay, the buyer commented: "George, the head of that buffalo looks too big for the body. Don't you agree?"

George studied the model carefully, and measured it with his calipers.

"I don't believe so," he answered, "it all measures out. But let's go out to the studio and check. I have the mounted head. Shot that buffalo myself!"

The buyer never afterward questioned the artist's research!

Phippen's paintings and bronzes now grace such museums as the Gilcrease Foundation at Tulsa, the Phoenix Art Museum in Houston, and The Art Gallery in Colorado Springs, Colorado. His paintings hang in homes in New York and Los Angeles, in Denver and Oklahoma City. Famous hostelries such as the Broadmoor Hotel at Colorado Springs and the Santa Rita in Tucson display his work, along with such collectors as Honnen of Denver; R. Q. Sutherland of Kansas City, Missouri; Richard Kleburg of the King ranch in Texas; and C. T. McLaughlin of Snyder, Texas.

Several museums, low on funds and slow in acquiring contemporary artists' work, are now casting about for Phippen art and will pay a premium for their past failure to recognize and commission work by this artist.

In the summer of 1964, the first organized showing of George Phippen's art was undertaken at Prescott, Arizona, in connection with their centennial celebration and annual rodeo. Museums and private collectors were scoured and loaned their Phippen art for the occasion.

About forty paintings and a dozen bronzes were shown, and Phippen experienced the first national wave of acclamation for his work. It was almost too late, for, all unknowing, he had then less than two years to live.

The showing was a tremendous success. One artist and writer of western themes, Clint World, wrote in the *Southwesterner*, "These paintings are so astonishingly beautiful that they take your breath. . . . "

George Phippen regarded his talent as a God-given gift that was bestowed upon him for his own happiness in the using, and in the interest of others. His nature was "unspoiled as a freshly-plucked peach," as Charles Comfort, Prescott newsman, said of him.

Though I never worked or rode with George Phippen, I have been told he was a fine horse breaker and a good roper. His paintings show that he knew every sinew, bone, and muscle in the horse, and was well acquainted with every piece of tack connected with riding them.

Less well known was the artist's ability to catch the moods and expressions of dogs, cats, barnyard fowls, and other domestic creatures. George owned a fierce wolf which he caged behind his house when we visited him. He was studying this animal, and also a bear that he had caged, sketching their expressions for some future work he planned. Only the genuine was good enough for him, no matter what the cost in time.

The greatest honor his fellow artists could pay him came to George in 1965 when The Cowboy Artists of America was organized and he was elected as the first president. The aims of the group, as set down in their constitution, are to perpetuate the memory and culture of the Old West as exemplified in the works of Russell, Schreyvogel, Remington, Bierstadt, Catlin, and others whose fidelity to truth was never questioned. The works that my friend George Phippen left behind him are a contribution to this ideal.

Following his last major operation, and from what we had all prayed was his convalescent bed, George sketched for his friends all through his long stay at the hospital. In cheerful little cartoon figures he depicted himself, Louise, and the hospital staff members who found themselves temporarily sharing his life. In one series of pictures, he had drawn himself mounted on his saddle horse riding the Rimrock in the Clouds and gazing over the edge. He appended this verse:

> I rode the Outside Circle,
> up on the Great Divide;
> But for your prayers and petitions
> I would have taken that long
> And Lonesome Ride.

It was George's last "Thank You," one he felt he had to write.

The world is always saddened when a great man, or a great talent, is lost to humanity. But when exceptional people just stepping into mature usefulness are taken from us, it is doubly tragic. So it is in the death of George Phippen, artist. Sadly, we will never know the true measure of genius that seemed almost certain to unfold in his full maturity.

Phippen's name will be enshrined in the heart of all Americans who love good and honest art, who treasure artistic integrity, and who take pride in their western American heritage. For George Phippen the artist was himself a product of this heritage.

15

Man In A Well

It took a strong body and a stronger faith in God, and his love for his family, to save Frank Carlin from the subterranean tomb into which he had accidentally fallen.

The team shied in the dusk, and Frank Carlin decided to investigate the trail road he was following up through the draw. He might be off the road.

Stepping from the spring wagon—and it was the longest step he had ever taken before, or since—he went into space, feet first. With the realization of what was happening, he raised his arms above his head, hands clasped together.

"Oh God, have mercy on me," he prayed as he plunged deeper into the inky blackness.

Frank Carlin had realized his plight almost instantly when he stepped into the void. He had fallen into a well. He knew, because he had helped dig some of those wells on the high tablelands of central Nebraska. Many of them, he knew, were 200 to 300 feet in depth. As the drought and grasshoppers of the early 1890s drove the homesteaders from their lands, they pulled stakes, leaving behind many abandoned wells. Open at the top, they were a deadly trap for both human beings and animals.

Carlin struck bottom like the dasher of an old-fashioned churn, splashing water and mud high. Strangling in the stagnant water, he brought himself to the surface and grasped for a hand hold on the casing. As he tore away bits of the rotting wood with his fingernails, he heard his team running away, carrying with them his sole chance of discovery and help from the outside.

The casing was slimy to the touch, but he managed to pull a rotting board from the curbing. With the benefit of a betterhand hold, he wedged the board into a groove between the other boards of the curbing and, with difficulty, fashioned himself a perch upon which he crawled.

Carlin was a deeply religious man. There was an affinity between him and nature and his conception of a living God. Like most settlers, he was also a rugged man, tough as rawhide, for it took tough men to live in that unfriendly environment. Now here, at the bottom of the abandoned well, sitting on the precarious seat he had fashioned, he took stock of his terrible predicament. Finding his greatest present asset to be his firm belief in the great, though mysterious, works of God, he prayed. After thanking his Creator for sparing his life, he turned to his physical condition.

One ankle pained sharply. It was already beginning to swell. Deep pains in his back told him of additional injuries, perhaps a broken rib or two. He was cold from the dousing in the muddy water, and the atmosphere at the well's bottom was fetid and moldy.

He looked up. The evening sky appeared as a tiny circle of smoky, star-dotted gray at the top of a column of black. Clinging there to his miserable roost, Carlin spent the night, cold and half-sick from his injuries, but mentally assessing his meager assets for the trials of the morrow. With God's help, he reasoned, he might yet emerge from the well alive. He had been spared, he knew, from instant death in his fall. Would God now help him from his living entombment?

When day stuck a thin finger of light into the gloom of the pit, Carlin commenced studying the well construction. The distance to the top appeared to be at least 100 feet. He little realized that the actual distance was 143 feet, and his underestimation of it, at the time, was actually a psychological asset to him. The well was curbed with tough cedar wood for distances of from six to sixteen feet. Then there were gaps not curbed at all. The curbing was tight. The three-foot lengths of cedar were a foot wide and an inch in thickness, not even providing space to insert a finger between them. The wood higher in the well was dry, hard, and well seasoned.

As Carlin groped for a means of scaling this tough wall, he came to the conclusion that his only hope would be to cut his way up the well curbing with his knife—if it hadn't been lost in his fall.

Reaching into his pocket, he felt for the knife. It was a good one with sharp, strong blades of good steel. Taking it out and handling it carefully to avoid dropping it into the water below, he began the chore of whittling out the first handhold and footholds for his ascent. The carving and whittling was slow, difficult, arduous work. It required a sharp knife point to outline and cut holes through the wood. But once Carlin had started, he never retreated.

During the first long day, he inched his way up the well side, carving first a handhold, then a foothold, then a crevice into which he could thrust the ends of his seat board and take some of his weight off his injured foot. At the day's end, when it grew too dark to work further without danger of falling or losing his knife, he fashioned a little better seat upon which to spend his second night. His strong and calloused hands were now blistered and bleeding. His throat was parched. His stomach cried out for nourishment. But he was fifty feet higher!

Throughout the night, the settler catnapped uneasily on his narrow ledge, getting what sleep and rest he could. His team, meanwhile, had been taken up by a neighboring homesteader and placed in a pasture. This good, but unimaginative, citizen had thereby complied with the technicalities of the law of that year (1895). He had notified the proper authorities of the stray stock, after impounding them in pasture. But with the impounding of Carlin's team he had, alas, also impounded the last possibility of discovery of Carlin in the well.

Carlin, of course, could know nothing of this as he huddled in the well, sleepless in his pain, hoping desperately that whoever found his team would start a search. He was cold and miserable and his feet now pained him intensely. The necessity for climbing mostly on his uninjured foot had now made that member almost as painful as the other.

The second morning brought grave doubts to Carlin. Looking upward, he could see how grossly he had underestimated the well's depth. He concluded that he might be in one of the giant 200-to-300-foot wells, since the distance he had progressed upward seemed so small relative to the great expanse still stretching above. The thought depressed him. For an hour or more he wasted valuable time calling for help. Only the echo of his lone voice answered, causing his stout spirit at this time to almost fail. But the recollection of his wife and his small son awaiting him at home spurred him on. With a fervent appeal to his Maker, whom he had almost begun to doubt, he resumed his toil.

Using sand from the well's side as a whetstone and with his own spittle, he brought the blades of his knife to fine points and sharp edges. Once again he attacked the tough casing. Patiently, he carved out handhold after handhold and foothold after foothold in the hard wood. Then, clinging against the well's side, he would carve still another handhold with which to drag himself up higher.

The hard clay in the uncurbed areas presented an even greater danger than the wood casing. The footholds in the clay must be deep; and to be safe, the handholds must be turned down at an angle to provide a solid hold for the one hand, while the other carved out the next hole.

By late afternoon of the second day, Carlin had reached a point less than thirty feet from the top. He was nearing exhaustion, and only his hardy pioneer constitution kept him from fainting and falling back into the well. And at this point, he met the greatest hindrance that he had encountered.

Above his head was a curbing, round and approximately four feet in height and perfectly smooth on the inside. Around its sides the walls had been eroded by rains at the earth's surface until the curbing hung suspended by a single peg in the side of the well. It dangled so insecurely above his head that he knew that even to touch it might mean crashing it down on himself and carrying him with it to the bottom. Carlin realized that to attempt to go up through it would be madness. He had been cutting through a similar earth strata less than twenty feet below and was impressed with the adhesive quality of the tough clay that had sustained his weight when he had mounted the sheer earth wall. Since he couldn't go up through the casing, he decided that he must carve his way up around it in the clay walls.

No doubt his mental and physical condition at this time conditioned him for the bold course of action he was to take. Audaciously, he cut a narrow ramp around the well's sides, avoiding the suspended curbing entirely! It was a most hazardous experiment and called for great ingenuity in bypassing the lone peg holding the curbing. Once this hazard was overcome and he had reached the remaining ten-foot curbing above, it was relatively short work to hack out the remaining handholds and footholds to the top, grasp the tough sunflowers that grew deep-rooted at the well's edge and pull himself free of the trap.

Carlin lay on the surface of the earth, exhausted. He knew that his escape had been little short of miraculous. When he had rested, he kneeled and thanked God for sparing his life.

Cutting a large sunflower stalk to use as a crutch, Carlin hobbled to the nearby deserted sod shanty, where he pulled off enough loose wood to cover the abandoned well. In the dusk of the evening he set off toward a neighboring settler's sod shanty. The following daybreak, after a night of hobbling and crawling, he appeared at the soddy of Charles Francis, where he was taken in, fed, and cared for by friendly and sympathetic hands—just two days and three nights after his plunge into the abandoned well.

Carlin's story became widely known among the settlers of the entire central Nebraska area and was largely responsible for legislation that brought about the covering and filling of the many abandoned wells in the region. Most settlers who were to stick it out through the drought years of the 1890s profited from this legislation, which enabled them to earn a few dollars filling up the old wells when money was as scarce as the grasshoppers were plentiful.

Truly, as Frank Carlin once said after his terrible experience, "God works in mysterious ways His wonders to perform."

16

The Sod House Photographer

He preserved images of the sod homes on the plains.

A sharp north wind blew down across the grassy plain of the Middle Loup Valley in Nebraska, causing the bearded man in the spring wagon seat to turn his head sideways to avoid its icy bite on his right cheek. On the side of the large, black box that had been built and bolted to the light wagon chassis was a hand-painted sign reading: "FOR T. J. AND S. D. BUTCHER'S PICTURE ALBUM OF CUSTER COUNTY."

The driver of the rig was Solomon Devoe Butcher, the "S. D. Butcher" of the sign. The date was 12 March 1899, the place, northern Custer County, Nebraska.

Butcher's team trotted with heads down, as though wearied by the long trip back from Round Valley where the photographer had been taking pictures that day of pioneer people and their sod homes. As he turned up the lane that led to his small frame home, his eyes widened with horror. A pall of smoke that had hung in the air for a short while, and which he had mistaken for a prairie fire that had been quickly extinguished, now became understandable to him.

The shocking truth came like an unexpected, paralyzing blow to the head; he felt sick. It had been his own home that was afire, and the black pile of ashes told the full, tragic story. As he drew near, a grief-stricken woman rushed over from the small group of people standing back from the smoking debris. Butcher pulled up the team.

"Great God, Lillie," he gasped, "what's happened?"

His wife threw herself into his arms sobbing quietly, unable to even speak of the loss she knew he had suffered. Their household goods had been burned to a crisp, together with their small personal belongings. But it was the large stack of now charred notebooks that had rested on his desk that she knew would be their greatest loss. For in those 100 notebooks her husband had carefully compiled 1,500 biographies of the pioneer people of the area, a work that had taken years of time and hundreds of miles of horse-and-buggy travel in all kinds of weather. The notebooks, together with the 1,500 and more glass plate photographs of farm and ranch scenes he had taken with his camera, were all now in ashes, scattered on the burned-over ground.*

Butcher placed an arm around his wife's shoulder to comfort her, and together they walked over to the smoking ruins as a neighbor led his team away.

"It's gone, Lillie, all gone." he said to her. "My history—my photo history—all up in smoke!" Tears slid down his bronzed cheeks as he thought of the great labor and time both he and his father had expended for the past thirteen years to gather this material. Now the work lay totally destroyed in the flames.

Solomon D. Butcher was born in Wetzel County, West Virginia, 24 January 1856. At age four, he moved with his family to La Salle County, Illinois. At age eighteen he had learned the photography business. For a few years he traveled as a salesman, but he was never without his camera, a large, bulky piece of equipment that used the old glass-plate formula and required most careful technical treatment, yet brought forth, for the dedicated, sensitive photographer, the finest of pictures. Butcher had learned the trade well, and was soon producing masterly photographs in that early age of photography.

In the spring of 1880, the Butcher family moved to Custer County, Nebraska, where his father, T. Jefferson Butcher, was one of the first to take up a homestead claim, just north of the Middle Loup River.

_____

*Amazingly, the following day, Butcher came across his glass plates, stored safely in another sod building! His notebooks, however, with all their information, were lost forever.

His father persuaded Solomon to file on a claim, too, but in a few months the photographer became discouraged with pioneer farm life and its hardships and left for Milwaukee, Wisconsin. There, and later in Minneapolis, Minnesota, Butcher attended Medical College, where he met and married a young widow, Lillie M. (Barber) Hamilton. The two made plans to return to Nebraska.

"I had seen enough of the Wild West to unfit myself for ever living contentedly in the East," S. D. Butcher remarked years later. And this was true for the great open prairies, the rolling hills of Custer County with their plentiful game and fowl and young, vigorous population had made its impression on Butcher as it had on many others who had absorbed its beauty and wild charm.

Back in Nebraska, near his father's homestead, Butcher set up his photograph gallery in a leaky sod house in which he and his wife lived. The venture was so discouraging and unsuccessful that the couple later moved to Walworth, a booming village a few miles east of the Butcher homestead. There, in 1886, the revelation came to him one day that he was witnessing a great change taking place on the prairie lands. New sod houses were beginning to appear on every 160 acres of the pristine prairie. Families of every nationality from Europe were moving onto the new land and from all of the eastern states and from the southern states, like Texas, where the cattle drives were bringing young men who wanted to stay in the north. The earth was rapidly being turned by the farmers' plows. The buffalo herds, the bands of elk and antelope were now gone. Only in the rough cedar canyons could deer and a few antelope still be found.

"In a few more years, Lillie, this entire land will bear a different appearance. Just thirty miles east of here, the sod homes are even now giving way to frame buildings. When the railroad gets to Broken Bow and lumber can be bought at lower prices, the soddies will disappear," Butcher explained to his wife. "That is why I would like to capture this scene on my glass plates as it is today, for people will find it difficult to even recall the pioneer and his way of life."

The flush of her husband's face told Lillie Butcher that her husband had truly seen a vision.

"Go ahead, dear, get pictures of all of these wonderful pioneer people, their homes and all that will reveal their life to younger generations," she encouraged him. "Show them just as they are. Make a true record of this frontier life we see now."

"A history book—a photographic history book of the sod house era," Butcher said, envisioning the title. "By Golly, that's it. We'll make a Picture Album of Custer County!"

S. D. Butcher's course was now indelibly set, one which he would follow through good times and bad, and many, many years before editors, photographers, and publishers of a later day would fully appreciate the great value of photography as a medium to record historical events.

"From the time I thought of the History Book, for seven days and nights it drove sleep from my eyes," he wrote years later in its pages. "I laid out plans and covered sheet after sheet of paper, only to tear them up and consign them to the wastebasket. At last, Eureka! Eureka! I had found it! I was so elated that I had lost all desire for rest. . . . I told my scheme to every one I met. I talked about it constantly. . . . "

Butcher's father offered to help him in every way possible, and the work began.

The first photo taken for the book was made on a summer day, 14 June 1886, at the homestead soddy of Elizabeth (Lizzie) Chrisman, daughter of a neighbor, Joseph M. Chrisman. Lizzie and her three sisters, Hattie, Lutie, and Ruth posed with their two saddle mares, Nellie and Daisy, before the rough sod home. From the Chrisman homestead Butcher drove to many more sod shanties on the plains, photographing the families and their homes and taking in trade whatever they had to offer—chickens, pigs, corn, or just promises to buy a photo and his book when it was completed.

When he was well along on the project he built the darkroom laboratory box on the back of the spring wagon to make instant developments. In this rig he and his father traveled to many of the far-flung ranches of the Great Sandhill country, as well as among the residents of Custer County, broadening the scope of his "picture album" to include most of central Nebraska.

The Spade ranch, J. F. Chappel's ranch, Stoll's ranch, John Good, Wysong brothers, Swain Finch, O. Keller, Austin and Son, John Cronin, the Ballard ranches, Dave Hannah's, Spall brothers, Rankin's ranch, the Ball ranch, and Bill Kennedy's ranch were among the scores of ranches visited where Butcher photographed the owners, their cowboys, cattle, rattlesnakes, coyotes, and anything else he found of interest.

Several years passed as he worked at his project. It had not been easy work. Times were hard and little money passed into his hands. His father's help was substantial, but Butcher was an independent man and did not like to draw on the older man's kindness unless he repaid him with labor in the fields. But the end was now in sight. He had written nearly 1,500 biographies from his field notes and had an equal number of photographs taken of these same pioneer people and their soddies and properties, as well as scenes of wildlife, Indians, cattle, horses, and other shots that had attracted his photographic senses.

In addition, where he could not get a firsthand photo of some historical event that had transpired, and which he thought deserving of recognition and remembrance, Butcher arranged reenactments of the scenes, including in the action men who had been actual participants in the events which had transpired many, many years before.

One example of Butcher's desire for authenticity is when he staged the hanging of the cattle rustlers, Mitchell and Ketchum, by members of the Olive ranch outfit. Butcher and a dozen pioneer farmers and cowmen rode to the Devil's Gap where the actual lynching took place; with the group was Al Wise, who had been with the cattlemen who found the bodies later, although he had not been with the lynching party. Wise guided Butcher to the exact location in a remote, treeless canyon that had been burned over by a prairie fire a few years before, eliminating the larger trees. The only remaining trees were now on the South Loup River two or three miles to the north. Wise sent two men back to cut a large branch, big enough to depict the small tree on which the rustlers' bodies were hung.

When the two men returned with the large branch, it was attached to the burned stump of a larger tree and the figures so arranged around it that the artifice would not be apparent in the camera's lens. The men were then grouped as Butcher suggested, and the picture was taken.

Al Wise, who did not want any misunderstanding of the fact that he was not a member of the original lynching group, refused to have his countenance in the photos but he did agree to pose with his back to the camera. So in the several pictures of the Olive-Mitchell-Ketchum tragedy taken that day, Al Wise is the man on the mouse-colored horse, always with his back to the camera, according to Butcher's son Lynn, who had heard his father relate the story.

By the year 1892, Butcher's work had progressed to such a point that he was fearful of missing some of the people who wanted their stories in the book, with scenes of their families and sod homes. So he advertised in the Broken Bow newspaper, the *Custer County Chief.* This is how he earnestly solicited their material:

> FARMERS: Have your farm photos taken by Butcher & Elwood for *Butcher's Pioneer History of Custer County.* A premium book offered for the best article from any part of the country, of 3,000 words or less, of the early settlement and up to date. Address me at Callaway.
>
> —S. D. Butcher

His father, T. J. Butcher, had become too busy to help much in the work so Solomon Butcher had enlisted the help of another photographer in order to complete the work, though only a few of Mr. Elwood's photos were reproduced.

At Callaway, Nebraska, Butcher received great help from George B. Mair, editor of the *Callaway Courier,* who agreed to receive the stories from the pioneers and help edit them for publication. But tragedy now intervened to halt production in the form of the great drought of the 1890s which fell across the land.

Butcher had waited and planned—and now had come this terrible, disastrous fire, almost on the heels of the drought, destroying his biographical sketches. Lillie wept again, and her husband was hard put to restrain his emotion.

As Butcher and his wife Lillie had poked through the blackened ruin of their home and the adjoining soddy they saw the bank of glass plates from which the photographs had been made. The plates were stacked neatly along the north wall. To give them added protection from the rays of light, Butcher had thoughtfully lifted two eighteen-inch pieces of fresh sod, each four inches in thickness, and laid them over the tops of the stacks of glass plates.

Lillie Butcher picked her way across the smoking embers in the yard and brushed some scorched sod from the top of the stacked plates. She lifted four or five of them from the pile, then ran quickly outside to lay them upon the grass, a few yards distant from the ruins, for the glass negatives were still almost too hot to handle.

As she carefully studied the top plate, the beautiful image of a newly constructed sod home stood out, visibly imprinted on the glass. Before the soddy, in the picture, sat the mother on a chair, holding her baby. Beside her, adding to the Gothic placidity and simplicity of the scene, stood her stalwart husband, holding by the bridles a fine team of mules. Three children, a boy and two girls, stood nearby, their bodies straight, their arms held tightly against their sides as they gazed into the camera lens. At the rear stood a hired man, standing bulkily beside a big ox team. Lillie Butcher cried out and ran quickly to her husband.

"Look, Daddy," she exclaimed, flourishing the bright image on the glass plate before his eyes. "It's *not* all gone! Your plates, your beautiful glass plates, they're all as good as new!"

Butcher seized the glass plates and studied them intently, holding them at arm's length above his head so the sun's rays could shine through them. He quickly ran across the fire's debris to view the stack of plates, examining them one by one. When he had satisfied himself that the glass negatives had been miraculously spared from the flames, he walked back to his wife and friends, holding a glass plate in either hand.

"It's a miracle," he said, shaking his head. "It's a God's miracle that so much of this work has been spared to me!"

Though the hundreds of biographies in his notebooks were destroyed by the flames, Butcher, working again with the zeal of a man possessed of a great idea, refinished the photos from the old plates that survived the fire. The result of his labor is the famous *Butcher Collection* at the Nebraska State Historical Society, and those photographs owned by collectors, the writer having some 400 prints from Butcher's original photo albums that were presented to him by the photographer's son, the late Captain Lynn J. Butcher, U.S.A. (Ret.), of Santa Ana, California.

When S. D. Butcher had selected the more than 200 photoprints he needed to illustrate his book, he and the editor, Mair, corrected the manuscripts and Butcher set out in vain to find a publisher. Engraving costs were high and there were 400 pages of text to be set on the linotypes. No publisher could be found to risk the venture. So near to his goal, with the book written and his photographs now ready, Butcher was more depressed than ever to again miss out on the successful conclusion of his long and arduous work.

One day, while near the South Loup River, Butcher visited the Swain Finch home and stayed overnight. Swain Finch and his good wife, Sarah, listened sympathetically as Butcher recounted the history he was writing and illustrating for posterity. That night when they retired, the Finches discussed Butcher's problems.

The next morning when Butcher had hitched up his team and was about to depart in his little spring wagon, Swain Finch followed him to the gate. Before Butcher had driven through the opened gate, Finch put down the post that held the barbed wire of the gate, then extended his hand to Butcher.

"Butch," the gray-haired cowman said, "you have worked hard on this history book—and faithfully, too. You *deserve* success! I don't pretend to know what the people of this country want, but, by George, if they want a history book, we shall see that they get it!"

These were the first encouraging words Butcher had heard for a year, and he rode away in his photographic laboratory spring wagon in high spirits.

Swain Finch was not a wealthy man, but he was a man with keen perception. He raised the money to underwrite the printing of the costly first edition of 1,000 copies of *Butcher's Pioneer History of Custer County, Nebraska*. If either Butcher or Finch made a penny's profit from the book it was another miracle. Certainly its author was never repaid for his great, and almost lifetime labor except in the renown that has been attached to his good name, and the prestige of his famous photo collection. His first edition was soon out of print and remained so for the next sixty-five years. The work reached a price of $75 a volume on rare book lists before its second publication in 1965. A third edition was printed in 1976, with another printing in 1979.

S. D. Butcher continued to be active in photography for several years with his son. When Capt. Lynn Butcher went to the war in

1917, Mr. Butcher sold their studio and entered the gas and oil field leasing business, scouting several successful fields before his death on 18 May 1927, at Greeley, Colorado. His body was returned to Custer County for burial and placed beside that of his wife in the little cemetery at Gates, Nebraska, within sight of the old Butcher homesteads he and his father, T. Jefferson Butcher, had claimed before the turn of the century. It was the region where he had received the inspiration for his life work on the illustrated *Butcher's Pioneer History of Custer County, Nebraska.*

In 1977, under the auspices of the University of Mid America, a group of ten midwestern universities, a series of six, thirty-minute segments of documentary film was made of the settlement of the Midwest. James (Jim) Wright, professor of history of Dartmouth College, served as senior historian for the project. The filming was done under the direction of Red Lynde, producer, of Melrose, Massachusetts; Frank Cantor of Boston; and Richard Camp of Wellesley, Massachusetts, handling the camera and sound. One segment of the series, "The Settlers of Custer County, Nebraska," drawing heavily on the Butcher Collection of photographs drew the distinction of winning the coveted Award of Excellence from the National Society for the Preservation of History.

The vision of the Butchers, father and son, gave to central Nebraska an enviable historical record in both pictures and text. One historian has commented that Butcher's history "is second to none." His is a record of pioneer life that is still sought after by historian and layperson alike, for it presents in the truest form a pictorial and factual portrait of the passing of the American frontier, written by pioneers and photographed by a man who was, himself, a pioneer.

17

The Bender Women—
The Damnedest Story
That Ever Was

The murderous Benders of Kansas caught!

> It has never been proved that the Benders were ever
> apprehended, nor is it certain that they made a successful
> escape.
>
> —*Kansas Historical Quarterly*

Introductory Remarks

Using the above quotation from the authoritative *Kansas Historical
Quarterly* (vol. 13, no. 2 [Summer 1957]: 146) as a springboard from
which to launch this story, one based in fact yet shot through and
through with folklore and legend during the passage of nearly one
hundred years since it happened, I shall attempt to bring before the
reader one of the truly gruesome, chilling, but thrilling tales that
came out of our early West during the settlement period.

The story of John Bender of Kansas, and his family, is known to
many. Probably not so well known is the story of the apprehension of
the Bender women, herein told. So well known was the Bender story
in Kansas, while I lived, worked, and researched there for fifteen
years, that I never did write it. But upon the invitation of the late Bill
Kostka, Denver, I gathered the accumulated materials to give you
what one writer has learned of the story. Be warned, however, that
this is a story with neither a happy ending nor a set of bracing morals.
Here crime pays, immorality thrives, evil wins out, and the foundation of law, upon which our western civilization is erected, crumbles

152

under the assaults of two lewd and lascivious murderesses. Our story, therefore, is written neither as history nor as truth, but rather as a sort of revelation in perversity, a subject which today seems an irresistible attraction to our average American reader.

In the early 1930s, *The Parsons* (Kansas) *Sun* published a series of articles about the Bender women. I learned that this series had been republished in 1952, and immediately ordered the file of newspapers in which they had appeared.[1] The series was written by Mrs. Frank Bailey of Chicago, the former Jean McEwen of Parsons, who had set down the mature thoughts of ninety-three-year-old Leroy F. Dick of Labette County, Kansas, a pioneer whose life had been inextricably wound up with those of the two infamous Bender women. Antithetical as was his own gentle nature to that of the two violent and bitchy trollops (the genealogy of which appears at the end of this article), Dick was never able to rid his own memory of their defiling influence and carried to his grave a detestation of their corruption. The story, unfolded by Dick through these interviews, bears the stamp of authenticity, for no mind, however inventive, could produce such an unfathomable account of pure wickedness and evil as is found in his account of the Bender women.[2]

* * * * *

Old Kate Bender was an ugly, malformed, and repulsive old hag. Young Kate, or Katie, was her physical opposite. Young Katie walked straight and tall, like a queen, her head adorned with a crown of carefully brushed red hair that fell around her square but delicate shoulders like a cascade of water, its rays reflecting the deep pools of her reflective eyes. Cherry-red, pouting lips and her olive skin attracted all strangers who saw her, and as the undemonstrative men of the Kansas frontier put it, "she's really sumpin' to look at!"

Though unlike in appearance, the two Bender women, mother and daughter, had many things in common. Both were cold and calculating murderesses. Both were thieves and pros. But let's wait and let the story reveal them.

No one knows to this day how many persons this murderous pair had slain—at least eight, the seven men and the small child whose bodies were exhumed within a few days of the Benders' departure from their Kansas home. Then there was Jones, a man whose body was found in the creek, and two more bodies found on the prairie after a blizzard—heads bashed in, throats slit. Unbelievably, the women had not been suspected until they left their scene of butchery. Only God knew how many murders they had committed elsewhere during their criminal existence on earth. One old man made a fair estimate of the pair. But few believed him. Once this old man, Leroy Dick, recounted his story to a young man who was a reporter. The artless fellow took this full cloth of what may have been truth and cut it up into a garb of fiction to fit his immediate need for a salable story. This aroused the old man and he never told the story again until he was ninety-three years old and knew he could not and would never write it down. Fortunately, Jean McEwen was there, and she wrote Dick's story in full.

The Bender family appeared in southeast Kansas, in Labette County, one morning in 1871. Near the old Indian Mounds, they selected a location for their home and unloaded their wagons. There were four in the party. Old John Bender, sometimes called William, was a beetle-browed, stooped old giant of a German with deep-set eyes peering from beneath bushy eyebrows; his wife was Old Kate. His son, young John (called Gieger), in his early twenties, was a tall, red-complexioned and rather handsome lad with a mannerism of attaching an aimless laugh to every comment he made. The foolish giggle prompted many who did not know him well to regard him as a half-wit. Young Katie was pretty, and she attracted men, which was her assignment in their business. To draw them to her with greater ease in a place that was Victorian in manner, if not in location, she circulated a handbill the following year that would make their presence at the Bender home and "grocery store" more acceptable to the community. It read:

Prof. Miss Katie Bender—
   Can heal all sorts of Diseases; can cure Blindness, Fits,
Deafness and all such diseases, also Deaf and Dumbness.
   Residence, 14 miles east of Independence, on the road

from Independence to Osage Mission one and a half miles
South East of Norahead Station.

June 18, 1872
KATIE BENDER

The neighbors soon learned that Katie also practiced spiritualism in
addition to her "medical" practice, and this added lure brought many
strangers to nibble at the fisherman, Death's, hook.

The Bender home was modest by even frontier standards, a former
school building of one frame room, occupied by the entire family.
Some shelving was built at the front and a small stock of groceries
displayed thereon. A sign over the front door read, GROCERIES.
Beneath the living quarters at the rear of the room was a small cave to
be used for winter storage of vegetables. A stone slab, with air space
below it for ventilation, was placed on the cellar floor. The cave was
provided with a trapdoor for winter access, and a tunnel led to the
outside from within the cave. Inside the single room a section of
canvas from the wagon jets had been draped across the room to
separate the living quarters at the rear from the front, which was their
store and the room where Katie Bender held her seances.

At the rear of the house were some small outbuildings and a corral.
A few fruit seedlings had been planted to make an orchard back of the
house, and young John had broken out a small piece of ground for
their garden. Here, in this lonely place with its rustic setting, the
Benders began their lives in Kansas. But the impact of this family
upon the tiny community would be so great that it would soon
change even the names of the Indian Mounds to "The Bender
Mounds."

Located as it was on the main road crossing Labette County, many
travelers passed this way, stopping to replenish their stock of tobacco
or groceries. Katie encouraged all males to stay overnight at their
store, enabling her to practice her spiritualism, as well as lighten
their purses for them. Though there had been few cases of missing
strangers along this route prior to the Benders' arrival, soon there was
an upsurge in the missing persons reports in this area. The discovery
of a man's body in a nearby creek caused some agitation to the
neighborhood. He had been foully murdered. Later two other bodies

were found on the prairie, heads crushed, throats slit. Their murders were discussed at the community meetings, but the Benders' name was never mentioned.

The sudden disappearance of Dr. William H. York of Independence Kansas, brought his brother, Colonel York, from Olathe, Kansas, to the scene with a posse of fifty men. York visited the Bender home and talked with Katie Bender. She admitted his brother had been there, made a few purchases, and traveled on. She willingly offered her services as a "spiritualist guide" to help locate the Colonel's brother, "even if he is in hell." But she begged the Colonel to return the following day, since her spirits were not cooperating at this particular hour. Her talk did not impress Colonel York with her intelligence, but it may have been the clue that touched off a later investigation, a most fruitful one.

Three weeks after Colonel York's visit, Billy Toll, a neighbor of the Benders, moved some cattle across Bender's claim. Billy was struck by the deserted appearance of the place. Finding the Bender livestock dead and dying of thirst and starvation, he hastened to the Harmony Grove Sunday School, where neighbors had gathered. There he told his news.

Leroy F. Dick, the man who lived to tell the story at ninety-three, was then a trustee of the township and constable. He immediately launched an investigation. Dick was a Civil War veteran and has been described among the *Kansas Historical Collections* as an honest and reliable man. At the Bender home he looked around the barn first, detecting the odor of decaying flesh. Though there was dead livestock at the barn, Dick was familiar enough with the odor of decaying human flesh to realize that it was not the recently dead animals that caused that particular sweetish-foul odor with which he had become familiar nine years earlier on the battlefields of the civil war. For once a man has smelled the decaying flesh of a fellow human, he never forgets it. Dick went then to his neighbors, the Sparks family, and they went to other homes, the Hornbacks, the McCrumbs, the Fergusons and the Douglases, gathering the men of the community to make a thorough search of the place, and to determine what had happened to the missing Benders.

When the group met at the Bender place, Ben Ferguson told Dick of an estray notice he had read in the *Thayer*(Kans.) *Headlight*, issue of 9 April 1873, just a few days before. The news story told of an abandoned team, wagon, and small dog, found near the village of Thayer. Among other trash and litter on the wagon had been found a board used for a wagon seat, with the letters, GROCERIES, painted upon it. Dick at once dispatched Ferguson and Maurice Sparks to investigate the news story, and the two men returned later with the information that it was unmistakably the Bender wagon and team.

The next day, the entire community being informed of the matter, about forty men appeared at the Bender place to conduct a search. The nearby creek and barns yielded nothing of interest, but the cellar under the house gave off such a sickening odor, and such a virulent one, that it became difficult to find men who would enter the cave and search it. When two hardy neighbors finally met the challenge with handkerchiefs wet with water tied over their noses, they found an abundance of putrescent blobs which Dr. Keebles of Thayer identified as human blood, clotted and mixed with lumps of earth. This news of the coagulated blood in the pit swept the settlement like a tornado and scores of spectators now gathered for the search.

Twenty-one days had now passed since the Benders had fled, and it had been about four weeks since Colonel York's visit. Now Ed York, a brother of the Colonel, who had been tied up with court duties, arrived on the scene. The search had finished in the house and cave, and now was centered at the rear of the house where the small apple seedlings had been planted. Recent rains had loosened the earth, and it could be seen that the ground had been harrowed over carefully, marks of the harrow-teeth still showing. Yet in places the tooth marks of the harrow were broken by telltale rectangular cracks in the topsoil, where the receding earth plainly indicated the site of a grave. Ed York, quickly noting this, ordered two of the men to dig at one of these marked sites.

After an hour's labor, the men reached a body. It had been buried nearly seven feet deep! Because of the decomposed condition of the corpse, the gravediggers objected to staying any longer in the hole. So Leroy Dick volunteered to go into the grave, remove the head, and hand it up for identification. Dick severed the head with a long, sharp, butcher knife and a pair of hoof trimmers. He washed the head with water handed down to him in a jug, then combed back the hair. Holding the head up to the edge of the grave he showed it to Ed York.

"Yes, that's my brother, Dr. Will," Ed said from between his clenched teeth.

Other searchers had continued digging into the cracked earth nearby, and soon another body was unearthed! This was the corpse of Henry F. McKenzie, a ne'er-do-well cousin of Leroy Dick's wife who had paid them a visit a few months before and had then left. They had not heard from him since he had departed, but thought nothing of it because of his irregular habits. Dick readily identified this body.

Once more the digging began. Next came the body of a Mr. W. F. McCrotty, from the Orange Mission. McCrotty had disappeared carrying a purse with nearly two thousand dollars in it. Following this exhumation came the corpse of another man, to this day unknown. Then followed the discovery of Benjamin Brown's body, a man from Howard County, Kansas. After Brown's body came a grave containing two bodies. The first was the body of Mr. G. W. Loncher, or Laugehor, as some accounts give it. Resting on top of the father's body was that of his baby girl, about five or six years old.

The discovery of the child's body brought macabre variety to the gripping scene. Now strong men's eyes were tear-filled as their women wept openly, for the child had apparently been strangled with her father's scarf. All the other corpses showed terrible head wounds, as though their heads had been crushed from behind with an axe, and their throats were slit in the same fashion as the bodies discovered on the prairie earlier.

A partially filled but abandoned well was almost encircled by the graves, and now the searchers went into it. Down seven feet, but covered with earth, they disinterred the body of a seventh victim, a John Boyle, or Bowles. This brought the tally up to seven men and the child, eight victims of as fiendish murders as had ever occurred in that area. Though the ground was probed over a wide area, no more victims were found, although it is possible others may have remained undiscovered.

Now the search turned to inquiring where the Benders had gone, for they had vanished as though into thin air. The story stated that the visit of Colonel York's posse had played a part—a most secret and sinister part—in the disappearance of the Benders. "The Benders never went any place, and won't be back," some of the local quidnuncs said with a wise look in their eyes.[3] And this know-it-all attitude held back community demand for a full-scale search for the Benders, for why look for those who are no longer alive, thought the members of the neighborhood.

Finding Bender's team in the nearby town and the uncovering of so many murdered victims soon brought Colonel York back with Col. C. J. Peckham, Henry Beers, and Marshall Jim Snoddy of Fort Scott. York quickly offered $1,000 reward for the Benders, but even his generous offer set further in the minds of many of the local people the impression that the Benders no longer existed, for many now felt that York would not offer such a large reward had not he, personally, known of their doom.[4] But Peckham, Beers, and Snoddy, with local money and encouragement, took up the dim trail.

The trio learned that the Benders had left shortly after Colonel York's visit to the Bender home. The railroad ticket agent at Thayer told them that the Benders had purchased tickets for Humboldt, Kansas, a town to the north of Thayer. The agent recalled a peculiar trunk they had with them, bound in animal hide, the hair side out, which was commonly called a "doghide trunk." At Humboldt the searchers learned that Katie and her brother had taken the MK & T Railway south, while the old couple had departed for Lawrence, and from there to St. Louis. At this time some folks expressed the belief that the young man, "Gieger," was Katie's husband, not her brother, and the searchers took this into consideration while following their trail.

The old couple's trail was followed to St. Louis. There a baggage smasher recalled the "doghide trunk" and also a white bundle the old Benders carried. A drayman contributed the information that he had delivered the trunk to a certain address. It proved to be the home of John Bender's sister! She confirmed the short visit her brother had paid her—the first in twenty years! Though she had tried to visit with them she found them uncommunicative and unsocial. While she was out shopping one day, they departed as silently as they had come. She thought their departure strange, indeed, under such circumstances.

Now the trail was cold, but the three searchers, Beers, Peckham, and Snoddy persisted. They checked the railway stations and the river docks. Beers wrote a discouraging letter back to Leroy Dick, indicating there was small chance of picking up a hot trail again. But a few days later at the St. Louis and San Francisco station they talked with a baggage master who recalled the doghide trunk. It had been shipped to Vinita, Oklahoma. Peckham and Beers hastened on to Vinita, but Marshal Snoddy had to return to his duties at Fort Scott.

Back in Labette County, Leroy Dick was now picking up a few loose ends of the case from a man who operated a boardinghouse at Denison, Texas, on the direct line southwest from Vinita. This man, Albert H. Owen, interested in the reward money, had come to Labette County, after meeting the younger Benders at Denison, according to his story. Dick was leery of "Bender stories" by now, for the case had attracted nationwide interest, and the usual assemblage of cranks and publicity hounds had tuned in on the affair. Yet Owens's story was so straightforward, Dick heard him out. According to Owens the young Bender had worked on a construction gang near Denison, with a team he owned. The young couple had left suddenly, Owen said, after making several inquiries of different men about an "outlaw colony" that existed down in the southwest part of the country. The young man had told Owens that the family was interested in "visiting" this colony and had appeared more interested when Owens told him that a law officer could enter that region only with difficulty, for it was populated with outlaws of all kinds.

Dick at once wired Peckham and Beers of this new twist in the trail, and the two searchers bought a team and a light rig and provisioned themselves for a long trip into the Southwest, pursuing the boy and girl believed to be the younger Benders. The trail was easy to follow for the first 200 miles, and they soon learned that an older man and woman had now joined with them. But as the ranches grew farther and farther apart and the roads crossed and crisscrossed in the wild cattle range country, they lost the trail again. Staying in the wagon ruts that remained to cross the rough and pristine country, the two men stuck it out through a labyrinth of tracks until they reached the Big Bend country on the Rio Grande River, just north of the Mexican border.

Here they hired a guide and wandered for a time through northern

Chihuahua after crossing the border. They finally recrossed near El Paso. East of El Paso, at a ranch house near Ysleta, they talked with a young horse wrangler who told them of meeting the four people resembling the Benders about a half-day's ride to the east. The wrangler took the two searchers to the fork where the Benders, if such they were, had turned off toward the outlaw country again. At this point, learning from the wrangler the great danger to their own lives if they rode into the colony, the two men gave up their search. They were out of provisions, their team thin and worn out. Peckham and Beers sold the team and rig at the next livery stable and returned to Kansas by train.

There was great disappointment upon their return. Colonel York expressed his disgust that the Texas government didn't wipe out such an obnoxious settlement, and he wired the Texas Rangers, as well as the authorities at Fort Sill, his complaints—bringing only messages of sympathy and information that surveys had not yet been run to determine where the colony lay or what might be its extent. So the Benders remained at a safe distance from justice.

No one knows how long the older Benders remained in the colony, but at some time they decided the interest in the Kansas murders had subsided to a point where they might set forth again to live in a more civilized community. But somewhere along the trail back to respectability, the old couple fell out and Old John, carrying the money bag, left the old woman to shift for herself. Young Bender, or Gieger, stayed and lived out his life in the Southwest, reports later said; a murderous life it was, as he took on the sobriquet, "Dutch Frank."

Katie stayed on several years in the colony after her parents left with the money. Eventually she departed from the outlaw colony with another young man, a painter, who deserted her when she fell ill at McPherson, Kansas. Here, Katie Bender came under the care of Mrs. Frances McCann, a young woman of excellent character and refinement, who was active in church work and in local Grand Army of the Republic circles.

One morning Katie was doing her washing at Mrs. McCann's home. Katie was very despondent and dropped the chance remark that it was "that damned old lady Bender" who had brought about her misfortune. Mrs. McCann was astounded. Upon questioning Katie she learned, to her amazement, that the infamous old woman, Mrs. John Bender, was Katie's own mother! But young Katie would offer no additional information at the time.

Frances McCann had been orphaned as a child. She told Katie that at least she knew who her mother was, and that was some consolation. Katie exhibited an interest in Mrs. McCann's life, and in the orphanage in Iowa at which she stayed. But to any further exchanges of confidence, Katie shut up like a clam.

A few days later Katie became seriously ill. Mrs. McCann stayed by her bedside and watched over her during her high fever and delirium. In her mind, Katie was again giving spiritualistic seances, and she repeated several times that she knew the true identity of Mrs. McCann! That, and the frequent assertion that "the Benders are very shrewd people," seemed to prey on Mrs. McCann's unconscious mind. Having no knowledge of her antecedents, or of her early youth, Frances McCann was most curious about Katie in some strange way and hoped Katie would lead her to more accurate knowledge about her own past.

When the fever left and Katie was stronger, Mrs. McCann told her of her statements in her delirium and asked her if she were able to reveal more about them. Katie studied the face of her benefactress and agreed that it might be good "to get it all out of my system." And with the revelation of Frances McCann's background, the story takes on one of those remarkable twists in which truth, in its weird unfolding, outstrips the wildest plots of fiction and where human credulity is stretched to the utmost.

Frances McCann's parents, said Katie, had lived in Windsor, Ontario, Canada. Since we shall never learn their names, we shall call them, for the purposes of this story, Helen and Paul Radford. As a small child, Katie had known the family. Just before Frances's birth, a woman with her sixteen-year-old daughter, whom Katie refused to name, came to nurse Helen Radford during her confinement. The unnamed daughter became violently infatuated in an adolescent way with Paul Radford, a handsome and kindly husband. When Paul tried to gently repulse her attentions, the daughter grew terribly angry at him and planned a bitter revenge.

One morning when the girl was in the basement of the home

slicing meat with a razor-sharp butcher knife, she cried out for Radford as though she were in pain. Radford came running down the stairway, alarmed by the girl's wild cry. She caught him in the throat with the knife blade, severing the jugular vein. Radford, shocked, and hardly realizing what had happened, died in great agony as he attempted to regain the stairway.

To prevent her daughter from being charged with the crime of murder, her mother concocted a wild story of a second man coming in the rear door and attacking the girl. Radford, she testified, was slain when he attempted to protect her daughter.

Frances McCann's mother, Helen Radford, died, said Katie, at the hands of the nurse or from the complications of childbirth—she didn't know which. However, the nurse and her daughter took the child, Frances, and left Canada for the United States. They lived in Kentucky for some time and later placed Frances in the Iowa orphanage while en route to Ionia, Michigan, to rejoin their family.

At this point Katie Bender's story came to an end, though try as she did Mrs. McCann could never get more information from her. About a week after this, Mrs. McCann found Katie packing a suitcase. She was going back to Michigan to find her mother, she told her, for she believed old Kate Bender must have some of the money out of which she had cheated her. Mrs. McCann tried to persuade the girl to stay, but it was no use. Katie left that afternoon for McPherson, Kansas— to be heard from later.

The bizarre story had left Frances McCann distraught. She pondered the fantastic tale for several days, yearning to learn more about her parentage. And she wanted to find, if humanly possible, her parents' murderess. Since the story had come from the lips of one who had admitted being Kate Bender's daughter, Mrs. McCann reasoned that Old Kate Bender might well be guilty of the atrocity. Certainly the old hag stood charged with enough other murders to her credit. Frances confided the matter to her husband. She had decided to go to Windsor, Ontario, in Canada to find out more about the murders, she told him, and to try to piece out the broken story Katie had told her. Understanding her anxiety, and sympathetic to her resolution, for he had been orphaned himself, her husband stood behind her. Soon afterward, Mrs. McCann left for Canada.

After a period of amateur sleuthing that tried her courage and her stamina, Frances McCann located a Mrs. Almira Griffith and her daughter, Mary, two lewd and lascivious females of the Michigan lumber camps. Searching into the womens' background, she found them to be the two women young Katie Bender had told her about—the nurse and her daughter responsible for the murder of Paul Radford!

The old lady was about sixty years old now, and this daughter in her middle forties. Mrs. McCann also learned that the Canadian authorities had exhausted all resources in attempting to gain a conviction of the pair in the Windsor murder case. She further found that Almira Griffith had been born Almira Meik, somewhere in the Adirondack Mountains. She had married a man, Griffith, when very young, and to them were born twelve children. While turning up her information on the background of this clan, she found lechery and lewdness in all forms. But the climax came for Frances McCann with the revelation that her own mother, Helen Radford, was the oldest daughter of Almira Griffith! And she, Frances McCann, was the old strumpet's granddaughter!

Putting her puzzle together, week by week and month by month, Frances learned that this unholy monster of a woman, Almira Griffith, had truly caused the death of her mother, Helen Radford, so that the sixteen-year-old daughter, Mary Griffith, might go free of the charge of murdering Paul Radford, for Helen Radford had learned the truth of her husband's death. And with these discoveries came the knowledge that Almira Griffith and old Kate Bender were one and the same person! It was almost more than Frances McCann could bear.

Back home with her husband, recovering from the implication of her several discoveries, Mrs. McCann tried to put her mental house in shape for the ordeal that must follow. She could not give up now, knowing what she had learned of the old strumpet, so she began to plan additional sorties into the enemy territory.

During the four separate trips she made to Canada and Michigan, ferreting out the past of Almira Griffith/Kate Bender, Mrs. McCann learned that a Flora or Florence was the third daughter of the old woman. Next came a son, William, followed by young Katie, whose real name was Eliza. The next two children, a boy and a girl, had died in infancy. Then came a son who was an epileptic. There followed three more daughters, Clara, Myra, and Ella, all living. A twelfth child, a girl, had also died in infancy.

Frances McCann returned from her third trip to Michigan in 1888. She brought back news that old John Bender had been hospitalized but upon recovery had once again disappeared. This information she turned over to the Labette County, Kansas, authorities. But her story seemed so fanciful that all agreed with Leroy Dick, who had been involved in the Bender story since its beginning, that Mrs. McCann's case could only be one of mistaken identity. A few reasoned that the orphaned Frances McCann was only trying, subconsciously, to build herself a family background, give herself a true mother and father, even if it had to be old Kate Bender and some unknown but surely dissolute Adirondack mountaineer.

Mrs. McCann stuck by her guns. She heard and knew what others were saying about her, but she refused to be swayed by idle and unsubstantiated personal opinions. Her husband supported her throughout her troubled times. She had seen the Griffiths, she told them. She had checked and rechecked her information. And the relationship with old Mrs. Griffith/Bender rankled her. The old harridan, she insisted, must be brought to justice.

In 1889 Mrs. McCann made her final trip to Michigan. Upon her return she came immediately to Labette County and talked with Bill Porter, who was the county treasurer. So impressed was he with her information that he urged her to go and see Leroy Dick. At Dick's home she told of the latest turn in the case. Both Old Kate Bender and young Katie, now calling herself "Mrs. Davis," were in jail in Berrien Springs, she said. If only someone from Labette County could now go up there, since they were in custody, and identify them, the pair could be returned to Kansas for trial. Witnesses could even yet be produced who would identify them, she told Leroy Dick. "People who have known and seen them, just like yourself."

Leroy Dick was still unconvinced and pled other business. Sheriff Wilson, being too old to make the trip, finally agreed to permit his son Bud to go and make the arrest. Many neighbors had by this time identified a photograph that Mrs. McCann had brought back as the picture of old Kate Bender, a photograph that had been taken of

Almira Griffith. But Mrs. McCann was not satisfied with the agreement to have the sheriff's son make the trip. The arresting officer, she thought, should be an older, more experienced man, one preferably who had known the Benders in life and could identify them. She asked the county attorney to step in, and at this time he called on Leroy Dick, asking Dick if he would make the trip. Dick objected strenuously, but when the attorney set up several photos on the mantel and asked Dick to identify old Kate Bender among them, Dick picked out a photo, one he knew to be the image of the old woman he had known as "Mrs. Bender."

"Are you positive about your identification?" the attorney asked.

"Yes," Dick answered. "I would swear that is a photo of the old woman Bender."

"That," said the Labette County attorney, "is the photo Mrs. McCann brought back, stating it was the image of Mrs. Almira Griffith of Michigan."

Dick was convinced. He at once prepared to make the trip to Michigan, using funds and identification the sheriff had prepared for his son to use. The Berrien Springs officers were notified by wire and in a few days Dick left for Michigan.

Leroy Dick first reported to the officials at Niles, Michigan, and then left for Berrien Springs where the two women were in jail awaiting trial. Sheriff Wrenn met Dick at the station and took him to his home. That evening he gave Dick a briefing on the Griffith family, assuring him that "Bender" must have been only an assumed name they used while in Kansas, for he had known of them for a long time. They were, the sheriff said, known over the entire southwestern section of the state, particularly in the lumbering areas as a whoring, thieving, kidnapping, lewd lot. They had been run out of many lumbering camps and towns in the area—Dowagiac, Buchanan, Three Rivers, White Pigeon, and other places where they attempted to nest. Flora, the weakling of the clan, whom the sheriff had hoped might talk, had disappeared. Done in by the old woman, he surmised. The law had never been able to make a conviction stick on them, he said.

Two of the Bender women were in the jail, just as Mrs. McCann had reported, the sheriff said. And they were engaged in an angry dispute between themselves. The old lady had received information that her name was being linked to the Kansas murders so she had trumped up a charge against Eliza, or Young Katie, as Dick thought of her. Eliza was going under the name of Mrs. Sarah Eliza Davis, the sheriff said. The old lady claimed Eliza had stolen some household articles from her. By this, she hoped to get Eliza in the toils of the law, to prevent her from being taken from Michigan back to Kansas. If the Kansas charges pressed in too close for comfort, the old lady then hoped to toss Eliza to the wolves while she escaped in the droshky, the sheriff thought. It was an Old World, peasant type of cunning, of which the sheriff was well aware. With this briefing, followed by a good night's rest, Sheriff Wrenn took Dick to the jail the following morning. Placing him on a stairway where he could view the two women, without being seen by them, Wrenn then talked with the prisoners while Dick listened and observed.

Dick studied the pair carefully, for it had been sixteen years since he had seen the Bender women and he wanted to make no miscalculation. As he watched he could see that the younger woman was unmistakably Katie Bender. The three-year-old boy she held in her arms startled Dick by his beauty. Young Katie, however, was aging, her girlhood beauty sapped by the years of dissipation. But there was no mistaking her image in his memory, red hair and all.

Until this time the old woman had stood with her back to him, but now Sheriff Wrenn worked her around until she was facing Leroy Dick. Here was the same old heavy figure, the same tossing of her head as she talked, the same old lumbering walk and the same mannerisms that had been those of old Kate Bender whom Leroy Dick had seen and known in Kansas. As she gestured at the sheriff, all these mannerisms now came back to Leroy Dick as a midnight dream, or fragments from a dream, sometimes return to one in the daylight hours. Dick knew that he could now swear on a Bible that these were the two Bender women, and he was suddenly aware of his shameful reluctance to listen to Frances McCann when she had implored him and others to hear her macabre story.

That afternoon the sheriff took Dick to the jail to meet the women face-to-face, introducing him as Mr. Wilson, a county commissioner from St. Joseph, Michigan. There was no indication of recognition on the part of the Bender women, and Dick was thankful to recall his reticence to visit the family after young Katie had made known her devotion to spiritualism, a practice that annoyed him and grated against his Christian principles. It had now paid off in their failure to recognize him. Only Old Kate's sly inquiry if he knew a "Mr. Peck" who lived in St. Joseph warned Dick that her suspicious nature was ever-present and that he must guard his tongue.

Before leaving the cell the old woman asked if she might have a word with the commissioner privately. The sheriff, of course, granted the request. When she and Dick stood alone in the corridor, she begged him to obtain a separate cell for her. She accused the younger woman of attempting to murder her. The younger woman, she said, was the infamous Kate Bender. She knew nothing of them, she told Dick, except—and here she pulled a newspaper clipping from her stocking! Dick glanced at the clipping. It dealt with the Bender case in Kansas, but why she had it, he could only surmise.

When the two returned to the cell, the younger woman laid her child on a bunk and asked the sheriff for permission to talk privately with the commissioner. Again Dick stepped out the door with Katie, or Eliza, and listened to her story. She displayed fright at being locked up in the same cell with her mother, and begged Dick to intervene with the sheriff and obtain a separate cell for her! The old woman meant to poison her and her baby, she declared, and further she identified the old woman as the infamous Kansas murderess, Old Kate Bender.

Dick had never encountered such diabolical duplicity. By their own introduction of the Bender murders he felt more certain than ever that he had apprehended the right persons and he hoped that somehow the two trollops could eventually be brought to justice for their fiendish crimes, possibly by using their confessions concerning one another. Assuming his role as the "commissioner," he asked the sheriff if two separate cells could be obtained for the women since it was to no one's advantage to have them murder each other when both seemed so near the gallows.

Before they left the Bender women, the sheriff questioned Katie about a man who had been murdered recently. "You knew him pretty well, didn't you, Eliza? What else do you know about that case?"

"Sure, I knew him," Katie quipped. "Slep' with him a few nights before. But I didn't kill him!" Katie flashed her toothy grin at the sheriff and rolled her eyes as though in jovial memory of the occasion.

"You seem to have had a lot of fun in your life," Dick observed to her. "You must have been a live one when you were a girl."

"Yeah," Katie said, spreading her full skirt before him and raising it to her knees so she could do a little jig for him, "But you know, the older the fiddle the better the tune!"

Old Kate joined in the raucous laughter with her daughter. Sheriff Wrenn grinned whimsically at the horseplay before him.

"But I always noticed that my fiddle needed more than one string!" shrieked the old woman, joining in the dance.

Dick addressed himself to Katie, ignoring the old woman.

"You enjoyed life when you attended my singing school at the Harmony Grove schoolhouse in Kansas, didn't you?" Dick asked. "Do you remember me? I'm the man who led the singing."

Katie dropped her skirt and ended her dance abruptly. She drew nearer to Dick. "I never knew you," she said darkly, her eyes narrowing as she studied Dick's face. For she had suddenly smelled danger. "I never laid eyes on the likes of you before."

"Well, I know you," Dick said. "I saw you both many times in Kansas." Now the old woman turned to Katie.

"You fool! I had a feelin' this man was from Kansas when I first heered him speak! And that he knew you when you were there!" The old woman stormed at Katie, but like a cat caught sleeping when rushed by a dog, Katie was on guard, her claws extended, her lips rolled up and hissing.

"What you mean—when *I* was in Kansas?" Katie shot back at her mother. "*You* were the one in Kansas—*you* caused plenty of trouble—you ain't lyin' your way out now and usin' me for a goat!"

The old woman turned to Dick, asking him to pay no attention to the frenzied charges Katie was now hurling at her. "She ain't got nuthin' to tell you."

"I can tell about that little nigger . . . ," Katie shouted.

"Shut your dirty mouth!" Old Kate screamed, raising a fist to strike her.

As the flood of accusations and recriminations flowed from the two hellions, Dick looked helplessly at the sheriff, and the two walked from the cell as the two wantons continued spitting their venom at each other. "It's like I told you," Sheriff Wrenn said as they walked down the corridor.

Young Katie's trial for larceny was held at Niles. The event brought a crowded courtroom, for the "Griffith" women were well known in the regional courts and jails. Mrs. McCann, having received a wire from Leroy Dick, was present at the trial and sat inconspicuously in the courtroom. The prosecutor's preliminary examination of Almira Griffith-Kate Bender produced the meager information that the articles stolen from her by her daughter amounted to as much as "fifty cents." This brought a laugh from all the spectators. Old Kate felt better, feeling the audience was now on her side, and she would make a farce out of her daughter's larceny trial, using it for a much more significant purpose—to pin the Kansas murders on young Katie Bender.

Katie's testimony was simply that her mother was lying, that she had been given the articles by old Kate. By accusing her of stealing the items, Katie pleaded, Old Kate hoped to get her mixed up "in that Bender scrape in Kansas," thus drawing the fire from herself.

The case seesawed back and forth, each woman trying to embroil the other in the Kansas charges. Old Kate hilariously testified to having had "twelve husbands—and in the market for twelve more!" She spoke freely of her whorings. But the prosecutor was able to find only one record of marriage, her first, and was never able to identify a particular husband, "a German I lived with in 1870 to 1873." Nor would the old woman admit to ever having lived in the state of Kansas. Dick and Sheriff Wrenn agreed that more must quickly be learned of Almira Griffith's husbands, otherwise nothing fruitful could come of the trial. So Dick headed for Grass Lake and Jackson, two towns where "marriages" had supposedly taken place. Wrenn returned the pair to the Berrien Springs jail until Dick's return.

Neither Jackson nor Grass Lake produced anything like a marriage certificate, although Dick made a thorough search through the court and church records. He did learn that the two women had been driven out of both towns, but not until the older woman had served a part of a term in the state penitentiary. She had struck a pregnant daughter-in-law (her oldest son, William's wife) a blow across the stomach with a club during a fit of anger. The baby died. For this, old Kate had been sentenced to nineteen years at hard labor. Given a new trial, she was exonerated and freed. With these findings, Leroy Dick headed back to Niles.

The larceny trial was continued, and the next testimony brought out of Katie that her mother had met a German in a logging camp near St. Joseph, had moved with him to Aurora, Illinois, and from there to Kansas. Katie also told of the vicious murder of a young negro girl by her mother. The girl had been a playmate of her sisters Myra and Ella, and the body had been hidden in a nearby slough. Old Kate had forced her to help dump the body, she said, then threatened her and held this over her head if she ever told. She was about ten years old at the time, Katie said. This was the first time she had ever revealed the murder, she testified. She had lived in terror all her life, and was deathly afraid of the old woman.

That evening after court adjourned, Wrenn and Dick drove over to Dowagiac to check up on the farmer that old Kate testified to having married there. There was no marriage record. The justice of the peace did provide them with the details of the farmer's murder, whose body was discovered afterward in the well. Old Kate had properly mourned his disappearance, then sold the farm. She was later indicted and held in jail at Dowagiac. Her epileptic son, just younger than William, was held with her, charged as an accomplice, for officials believed he might turn state's witness. Old Kate warned the officers that her son might die in jail without medical attention. He did, fortunately for his mother. Most of the officials believed old Kate. With the chief witness who could have testified against her now dead, she was freed "for lack of evidence."

At the next session of court, Katie testified that she knew the old woman had poisoned the boy and had killed the farmer to inherit his property. The boy had been made to help her throw the body in the well, Katie said, and she offered the evidence that old Kate had murdered many other people including "those people out in Kansas." Old Kate and the old German man had made a lot of money from murder, Katie insisted.

Leroy Dick, a mild-mannered man who had never believed that

crime paid, and who had scrupulously obeyed the law as well as enforce it, shuddered at the words coming from the two vituperative murderesses, each fighting mercilessly for her own life, each remorselessly willing to sacrifice the other. That day he took the train to Flint, searching again for the old woman's unrecorded marriage licenses, not a one of which he ever unearthed.

During the trial, the old woman had said that her daughter, Mary, lived in Saginaw. This was the daughter who, as a girl, had murdered Radford. From Flint, Dick journeyed to Saginaw to visit with her. He found Mary a big woman, now married successfully to a man of Italian descent. Mary wanted no part of her mother's problems. The big daughter knew nothing of her mother's marriage to a German, but suggested that a sister, Clara, living at Muskegon, might have information about him. Dick thanked Mary and hurried on to Muskegon.

Clara was cooperative, thinking that the information might some way help her mother out of another scrape with the law. She could not recall the German's name, but he had lived with her mother from 1870 to 1873, she recalled. Eventually the name of the German came to her mind—John Flickenger. Clara recalled her extreme distaste for Flickenger; the reason she thought she had remembered his name, was because he had once thrown one of her own "husbands" bodily from the house. Dick departed, well-pleased at his new information.

At St. Joseph, Dick again searched for the elusive marriage certificates. No luck. Nor did he turn up one in the state of Michigan. The local authorities knew of the Griffith women, of their "baby farming" (selling kidnapped babies) and whoring. Lawmen once thought they had evidence to convict the old woman by pressing Florence, the weakling of the family, to testify against her. Florence disappeared under peculiar circumstances and once more the officials believed the old woman had murdered a daughter to cover up her own trail of crime.

Dick returned to Niles, and with his new information they now felt they could make the old woman talk. The following day the prosecutor fenced with the old bawd, awaiting the proper moment to score the touché and make her admit that she lived in Kansas with old John Bender in 1871 and 1872, he being known in Michigan as John

Flickenger. But when the moment came the old woman only made the lame apology that she had so many husbands she had forgotten this one. But she never admitted to having lived in Kansas.

Dick had previously made arrangements with the court and the district attorney to remove the two Bender women to Kansas without requisition, or extradition procedures. Katie was summarily acquitted of the larceny charge and the following day Dick put the pair on the first train south, lest by delay Michigan officials might decide to hold the pair and charge them with the Kansas murders and try them in Michigan. The old strumpet and her daughter fumed and fussed at Dick, but became reconciled to their return to Kansas.

At South Bend, Indianapolis, and St. Louis, reporters boarded the train to question Dick and interview the women. All during the trip they were the subjects of curious eyes. At Nevada, Missouri, Katie came tripping back from the washroom to inform Dick that when they reached Kansas they would have a top lawyer. What she would use for money, Leroy Dick could not conceive, so he sat with concealed amusement, wondering what satanic imp within the woman drove her to try to create a sensation when her own life was at stake.

Dick wired ahead to Sheriff Wilson and he and other officers took charge of the prisoners. The preliminary hearing was held in Judge Keesy's court. To Dick's utter surprise Katie's "top-notch" lawyer was there. He was John T. James, and it was soon apparent that he knew his way around court quite well. It had now been sixteen years since the Bender victims had been exhumed from their graves. Many old settlers who knew them had passed on, and others had moved away. But there were enough living witnesses to identify both of the Bender women. The elder Dick, Father Dienst, Maurice Sparks, Rudolph Brockman, Ben Ferguson, Leroy Dick's brother Temple, Mrs. Delilah Keck, Jim McMaim, Bob Campbell, Tom Finley, Henry McKean, William McCramb, and a Mr. Ratliffe were there. Many of them had known the Benders by sight. Some, like Leroy Dick, had been present when their victims were unearthed.

James, the attorney for the defense, asked for the services of another lawyer, Judge H. G. Webb, to aid the defense.[5] John Morrison was the prosecuting attorney. The hearing opened, and when the question "Do you recognize these women as Mrs. John Bender and her daughter Katie Bender, who lived here from 1871 to 1873?" was asked, seven of the witnesses answered "Yes." Six of the remaining witnesses thought the pair resembled the Benders, but could not swear they were actually the same persons. Still other witnesses unable to attend the preliminary hearing identified the pair from photographs.

Upon this testimony, the court conceded their identity, and on 19 November bound them over for trial to be held in the district court, May 1890. As the constable took charge of the pair, he overheard old Kate remark, "My, didn't Mr. Dienst look natural, Eliza? And old father Dick is lookin' awful well for his age."

The trial of the Bender women produced as many quick turns and surprises as had their apprehension and extradition from Michigan. As a first bombshell on the prosecution, the defense lawyer turned up with as good a marriage certificate as one would ask to see, made out at Jackson, Michigan, and purporting to show that Almira Griffith had married a Mr. James there in 1872! The court held the certificate to be authentic. Dick fairly moaned, for he had searched the town with a fine-tooth comb and found nothing like a marriage certificate. Later, he called the certificate a rank forgery. But the defense lawyer had only begun.

Next, John T. James exploded a time bomb he had set and charged earlier. This was a prison record showing that Almira Griffith was serving a prison sentence in Detroit at the time of the Kansas murders! Leroy Dick's case, strong as it had appeared to him earlier when the women were identified as the Benders, now collapsed. The prosecutor, John Morrison, convinced of the state's inability to gain a conviction after that, dismissed the case.

Dick still held hopes that some event would arise to yet bring the pair to justice. Not long afterward he met the Parsons, Kansas, chief of police on the street. "Well," the chief remarked, "I see your birds flew the coop." It was true. The two women had been freed from the jail and the police chief had observed them as they walked down the street, the one called Eliza pulling the small boy in a little red express wagon. Some well-meaning folks had provided them money to take them as far as Fort Scott, though the state had provided them both money and transportation home!

Leroy Dick sat down on the board sidewalk, overwhelmed by the turn of events. It seemed incredible to him, and the chief of police sympathized, urging him to go over and talk to the district judge about the matter. But at the judge's office it was the same. "Yes, they have been discharged," the judge told him. "There's nothing that can be done now."

Two months passed. One day as Dick sat scanning the newspaper at his home, his own name caught his eye. It was a news story stating that Leroy F. Dick and the county of Labette, Kansas, had been named the defendant in a suit for the recovery of $10,000 damages "to the reputation of one Almira Griffith!" Dick nearly hit the ceiling. At Oswego the following morning, where he had gone to get the particulars of the lawsuit, he came face-to-face with old Kate Bender-Griffith, and Katie, pulling the small red wagon with the boy smiling at passersby as he rode upon it.

"Eliza!" Dick exploded, "what in Heaven's name are you two trying to do?"

"You caused us plenty trouble, now we're a goin' to fix you," her mother answered with spite shooting out of both eyes. Dick turned to old Kate.

"You go right ahead," he said quietly, "for this will give me my last and only chance to put you both in the penitentiary." At Dick's own show of belligerency, the old woman retreated.

"We had to do something," she whined. "We're broke and got to live, ain't we? I tole Eliza she oughtn't try to ruin the reputation of a nice, respectable man like you." Katie glared at her mother.

"You damned ole liar, you're the one who egged me into doin' it!" she screamed.

Dick abruptly broke off the conversation and left, feeling nauseated. At the constable's office he learned that the defense attorney had rushed back to town, ordering the two to call off their lawsuit as soon as possible. He had saved them once, he told them. That was enough.

A half a century and more of time has now passed. At the age of ninety-three Leroy Dick sat one evening in his study, the Bible on his lap. It had been more than fifty years since he last saw the Bender women. He reflected on life, and how his own later years had been influenced by the Bender women, and old John Bender.[6] As he turned the pages to the prophet Jeremiah, a passage he had pondered many times before came to his eyes:

> Nay, they were not ashamed. Neither could they blush; therefore, they shall fall among them that fall. At the time that I shall visit them they shall be cast down, saith the Lord. . . .

Dick's eyes turned from the book to the serene face of his own good wife, gazing down upon him from her photograph on the mantel. A feeling of peace came over him. Glancing down once again to the words of the prophet he said softly to himself, "Yes, surely, this must apply to those such as the Bender women."

Notes

1. Mrs. Frank Bailey, "The Bender Hills Mystery," *Parsons* (Kansas) *Sun*. See issues of 11–18–25 October; 1–8–15–22–29 November; and 6–13 December 1952. The series was first published in the *Sun* in 1934.

2. Scores of articles concerning the Benders in Kansas have appeared in many magazines and newspapers in the United States since the atrocious murders of 1872. Examples are Alan Hynd, "Killer Kate," *True Police Cases* 12, no. 123 (April 1960), and Edwin V. Burkholder, "Those Murdering Benders," *True Western Adventures* 3, no. 12, (February 1960). Burkholder was the late editor of *Real West*. Only these two are mentioned, for a complete listing would fill a page or more.

3. That Colonel York and a posse did find and execute the Bender family is doubtful, for had he done so the execution would have been without proof of the Benders' guilt (there had been no *corpus delicti* shown) and had the Benders confessed their guilt, as is sometimes averred, the posse would have immediately returned and exhumed the bodies.

4. In *The Chronicle News*, Trinidad, Colorado, issue of 21 July 1908, p. 4, the author turned up the story from the lips of a Colorado man who alleged he was a member of the posse that executed the Bender family. He was George Evans Downer, born 1 February 1847, in Beloit, Wisconsin. Downer was a veteran of the Civil War at age seventeen, with the 47th Wisconsin Vol.

Infantry. According to his story the posse overtook the entire Bender family, fleeing from their home in Labette County, Kansas. In a running gunfight, north of the Bender home, old John Bender was shot and killed and fell from the wagon. "Geiger," or young John, as he called him, jumped from the wagon to escape and was killed. The old lady Bender was shot and killed on the wagon. While the posse was burying the three dead members of the family, together with one of the posse members who was killed (unnamed), young Katie Bender was untied "as she agreed to tell the truth." Katie told of the murders of York and the others. Then she grabbed a gun from a man, but another posse member shot her "directly between the eyes." The posse members swore to never tell of their actions, but then returned and dug up the victims' bodies. The only posse members' names recalled by Downer were Whitney and Brown. He also thought a banker from Independence named Page was with the posse, and possibly a man named Delos Avery, to whom Downer gave his Derringer pistol when he left Kansas. Downer listed the bodies found as Dr. William H. York, G. W. Langchor, Langchor's child, Benjamin M. Brown, John Greary, W. F. McCrotty, and H. F. McKegzie. (The spelling is as Downer gave the names.)

5. There is a book on this subject and lawsuit, written by John T. James, the attorney for the defense, titled *The Benders in Kansas* (Wichita: Kan-Okla Publishing Co., 1913). In this work, James summed up the case:

> The abnormal desire to be known as a notorious criminal and the unbridled tongue of Sarah Eliza Davis, whom one of the attorneys for the defense in his address to the Court said was the "most colossal liar" of his experience in criminal practice, had caused these defendants all this trouble and laid the base for the enormous expense which had been made to arrest and prosecute them as the alleged Benders.

6. Dick learned later old John Bender had been accidentally drowned in a Michigan lumber camp not long after his hospitalization which Frances McCann reported after her return from Michigan in 1888.

Genealogy of the "Griffith" Family

All names appearing in the story, with the exception of Leroy F. Dick and those of the other honorable citizens of Labette County, the members of the trial court, and the Bender family— Old John, his wife, Katie, and "Gieger"—are fictitious and are used herein to protect the descendants of Katie Bender who may possibly, though it would seem doubtful, have lived circumspect lives.

Almira Meik   married   _____ Griffith
(born ca 1828)   (ca 1842)   (an Adirondack mountaineer)

|

Issue:

1. Helen, born ca 1843. Frances McCann's mother, Helen Radford. Slain ca 1860, the year Frances was born.

2. Mary, born ca 1844. Murdered Paul Radford.

3. Florence, or Flora, "the weakling," born ca 1847. "Disappeared."

4. William, born ca 1849. Almira Griffith killed his pregnant wife about 1866.

5. Eliza (Katie Bender), born ca 1852. "Mrs. Sarah E. Davis." She lived in Ionia, Michigan, about 1862 when she was ten, and was about nineteen when in Kansas.

6. Boy, unnamed, born ca 1853–55. Died in infancy.

7. Girl, unnamed, born ca 1853–55. Died in infancy.

8. Boy born ca 1856. Afflicted with epilepsy. Died in jail under peculiar circumstances during trial of his mother for the murder of her husband, the farmer found in the well.

9. Clara, born ca 1858.

10. Myra, born ca 1859.   They played with the small Negro
11. Ella, born ca 1861.   girl slain by Almira Griffith in
                           1862–63.

12. Girl, born ca 1864. Died in infancy.